POCKET FULL *of* VICTORIES

POCKET FULL of VICTORIES

New Life, New You and New Victories in **Christ**

by:

TANEKI DACRES

THE VINE PUBLISHING

Copyright © 2011 by Taneki Dacres.

All rights reserved. Except permitted under the U.S. Copyright Act of 1976, no part of this publication may be used, reproduced, distributed or transmitted by in any form or by any means, graphic, electronic or mechanical or stored in a database or retrieval system, without the prior written permission to the publisher except in the case of brief quotations embodied in critical articles and reviews.

Cover Image: © kohy – Fotolia.com

Unless otherwise indicated, Scriptures are taken from the New King James Version.

Copyright © 1979, 1980, 1982, Thomas Nelson, Inc., Publishers. All rights reserved. Used by permission.

Scriptures noted NIV are taken from the Holy Bible, New International Version®, NIV® Copyright © 1973, 1978, 1984, 2011 by Biblica, Inc.™ Used by permission. All rights reserved worldwide.

Scriptures quotations marked AMP are taken from the Amplified ® Bible.

Copyright © 1954, 1958, 1962, 1964, 1965, 1987 by The Lockman Foundation. Used by permission. (www.Lockman.org)

Scripture quotations marked NLT are taken from the Holy Bible, New Living Translation. Copyright © 1996, 2004, 2007 by Tyndale House Foundation. Used by permission of Tyndale House Publishers, Inc., Carol Stream, Illinois 60188. All rights reserved.

The Vine Publishing Inc. books may be purchased through booksellers or by contacting:
244 Fifth Avenue,
Suite T296, New York, NY 10001
www.thevinepublishinginc.com

ISBN: 978-0-9856535-0-7 (paperback)
ISBN: 978-0-9856535-1-4 (e-book)
ISBN: 978-0-9856535-2-1 (hardcover)

Library of Congress Control Number: 2012944233

Printed in the United States of America

THIS BOOK IS A GIFT TO:

_____
Recipient

From:

_____

Date:

_____

DEDICATION

Pocket Full of Victories is dedicated to my beautiful mom, Lorna.

Mom, thank you for not only being a great mother, but thank you for also being a best friend. Our bond has been impenetrable and unbreakable. Your unconditional love and support has been a true comfort to me throughout the years.

Words cannot express my gratitude for you. You have been there through thick and thin. You have been my personal cheerleader, always cheering me on and encouraging me to pursue my dreams (regardless of how grandiose they were).

Mom, thank you for simply being my mom. I love you so much and I appreciate you.

Thank you. Love you mom!

CONTENTS

ACKNOWLEDGMENTS		I
PROLOGUE		III
PART B	On The Fence	23
POCKET 1	Abba's Child	53
POCKET 2	You Win!	69
POCKET 3	Mind Games	87
POCKET 4	Watch Your Mouth!	103
POCKET 5	Sweet and Sour	119
POCKET 6	The Good Fight	137
POCKET 7	Super Enabler	177
POCKET 8	Arsenal of Victories	205
POCKET 9	Blessed Vessels	239
POCKET 10	Closing Remarks	259

ACKNOWLEDGMENTS

I first have to acknowledge and thank my Lord and Savior, Jesus Christ for anointing me to write this book, without Him I am nothing. Lord, I give You all the glory, honor and praise. I love You and thank You.

A special thanks to my mom, of course! Again, I love you mom (one can never say it too often). To my stepfather, thank you for being my example of what a good father should be. Grandma, thank you for your love and wisdom. Thanks to my family for all your love, support and prayers, especially when I needed them the most. Thank you so much to my spiritual mother, Rev. Jenifer Fisher, for your prayers, spiritual guidance and love. To my sisters in Christ, I love you and thank you. A special thanks to Tanesha Lawrence, you have been more than a friend to me; you have truly been my sister. I love you and thank you for your support.

There are so many people to acknowledge and I could go on and on but, let me just say: Thanks to everyone who has supported, encouraged, prayed for and simply loved me. Please know that I see you, I appreciate you and I love you. God bless.

~ *Taneki Dacres*

PROLOGUE

TANEKI DACRES III

The year was 2009, and I was loving life. I wasn't completely where I wanted to be yet, but I was on my way. I had a vision; I had plans. A few years back I had sold my sandwich shop franchise restaurant, done a little traveling, moved back in with my parents, and regrouped. Now I had a new business venture and it was going to be great! I knew it—I just felt it. Yes, this would be the BIG one. I could see it: new venture, success, marriage, children, complete bliss, retirement, and death. Yes, I had plans. What's more, I had finally found a church where I felt comfortable, so when I wasn't too tired, I'd squeeze in a service from time to time. All was well. My launch date was in the middle of the Christmas holiday season, which was coming up and I had to keep my eyes on the prize. There was no time to waste—I had to focus.

October 2009, three months to the end of the year, and I was extremely busy. Everything was falling into place and I kept pushing towards my goals, but in the midst of my hectic schedule I began feeling lethargic, not as energetic as I would have liked to be. Thinking that my doctor may be able to prescribe some super-vitamin to kick my body into motion, I scheduled an appointment. Blood work: Check! Wait for results: Check! Results: "Your blood count is 4.5. You are severely anemic." My thought: "Isn't everyone anemic? Most people I talk to say that they are. What's the big deal? Now I'm just one of them." As severely low as my blood count was, I opted out of getting a blood transfusion, was prescribed high doses of iron pills and went back to business as usual.

Okay. I still had time to launch this business for the holiday season. I had to focus, but for some reason I just could not shake this lethargic feeling, and to make matters worse, I was now experiencing shortness of breath. Plus, every night, I was awakened by a piercing headache, a pain I'd never felt before. I didn't want to do it, but I knew it was time for a visit to the emergency room.

I dreaded the emergency room—long waits, sick people everywhere coughing, bleeding and in pain. It was my worst nightmare, but I had no choice, and I went. Blood work: Check! Results: same diagnosis—severely anemic. The doctor said, "I can't guarantee what would happen to you if you leave here without a blood transfusion. Your heart could stop at any time due to the low blood supply. Anything can happen." And with that grim picture, I agreed to get a blood transfusion. After all, I had plans, and I liked the idea of living to see another day. I recited a quick prayer and off I went.

The transfusion was in progress. But, as soon as blood started flowing into my veins, my left leg began to cramp. "Doctor," I said, "my leg is cramping." The doctor answered, "Oh, that's probably a sign of the anemia." Okay. He went to medical school; surely he knew what he was doing. "Suck it up, Taneki!" I told myself. "Remember: You have a business to launch soon." Finally, transfusion completed and I was discharged from the hospital. Back to business as usual—well, not really.

The day after the blood transfusion, I began to feel sore in my upper back, then in my lower back. This prompted me to call the hospital: "Hi, I received a blood transfusion last night and was told that I should call if I felt that I was having any reactions to the blood. Well, I'm sore in my upper back. What do I do?" The nurse said, "Take an aspirin." Okay. Surely he knew what he was talking about; he went to nursing school. "Suck it up, Taneki!" I told myself again. "Remember: You have a business to launch soon." As the days went by and I attempted to get back into the swing of things, I began to notice that instead of soreness, I was now experiencing intense pain in the lower-left part of my back. *Take an aspirin. Keep it moving. Stay focused.*

Days turned into weeks, and it was now November 2009—two months before the end of the year. I could see the finish line, but unfortunately the pain had worsened. It was beginning to be unbearable. At this point, I could hardly lift my left leg, and on top of that, I was experiencing severe shortness of breath. This was not the same shortness of breath I had experienced before—no, this felt like every breath I took may be my last. I had no choice at that point. I had to see my doctor immediately.

It was only by the grace of God that I made it to my doctor's appointment. I had to drag my left leg up each subway step, stop, try desperately to catch my breath, and start all over again before I was able to reach the top of the platform. Eventually, I made it to my appointment.

Blood work: Check! Results: "Everything seems normal, and your blood count is great." Hoping to avoid another visit to the emergency room, I made an appointment for the following day to get an X-ray of my chest. "I can't believe this is happening to me!" I thought. "I have plans. And this pain and shortness of breath are *not* a part of those plans!"

The next morning I jumped out of bed, ready for the day. I had scheduled the X-ray appointment for the evening so that I could help my mom take my grandmother to the hospital for a medical procedure related to her bladder cancer. As I began to get ready, I began experiencing the most severe shortness of breath yet. I tried to shower, but it felt like I would lose consciousness at any moment. Out of sheer panic, I kept hitting the walls of the shower, fighting desperately to breathe. I began to cough, fighting desperately for a single breath, fighting desperately to live.

I eventually got out of the shower, and with every movement, I lost my breath. I could hardly walk or talk and barely got my clothes on. I knew that something was seriously wrong, and that if I didn't immediately find out what it was, I would not be alive for very much longer. I can't explain it, but I knew that death was swiftly approaching.

Out of my desire to emotionally support my mom and my grandmother, I eventually made it to the hospital, but things quickly took a turn for the worse, and I was wheeled from my grandmother's bedside to the emergency room for tests. "*Ahh.* The dreaded emergency room," I said to myself. X-ray of chest: Check! Results: nothing unusual. Ultrasound of legs: Check! Results: nothing unusual. "Oh Lord," I prayed, "please don't tell me that this is going to be like an episode of *Mystery Diagnosis*! Am I dreaming? Because all of sudden, lying here in the ER, I'm not feeling so bad. Will I be sent home only to come back years later and find out that I have some rare disease? Oh Lord remember my plans!" As if the doctor read my mind, he said, "Don't worry. You're in the right place and we are going to figure this out. If we see nothing on one test, we'll move on to the other." "Okay," I thought, "that's more like it. Let's continue then."

CAT scan of chest: Check! Results: pulmonary embolism. "Pulmo—*what?*" I asked. The doctor said, "You have impressive blood clots in both lungs. You are very lucky to be alive, and we have to admit you." (I now know that "impressive" is the word doctors use when they want to say "out of this world!"). Needless to say, I was dumbfounded and devastated.

All I kept hearing from doctors was, "You are very lucky." One doctor, after looking at my reports, said in her amazement, "The last time I saw a case as severe as yours was years ago, early in my practice. We tried giving the patient blood thinners, but after a day or two she died." She kept asking me if I'd seen my own reports and if I knew how lucky I was to be alive. But, I knew that luck had nothing to do with it. I knew that it was God, the grace of God that saved my life. The same God I prayed to from time to time (when I wasn't too tired); the same God I knew *of* but didn't really *know*; the same God that I'd never felt the need to commit to—He saved my life. Luck had no part in this.

Well, so much for my "plans." It's funny how God works. There is an old saying that goes, "Man makes plans, but God wipes them out." Now, while I don't completely agree with this, I've now come to understand that our plans may not be His plans for us. And, at the end of the day, His plan will be executed. He may have to drag us kicking and screaming through sickness, trials, and tribulations. Regardless, He will get His way and His purpose will be done.

A few days shy of three weeks, on Christmas Eve 2009, I was finally discharged from the hospital—just in time to have a real home-cooked meal with my family. I couldn't be happier: real food! At this point, the new business venture and all my other plans were far from my thoughts. I was grateful, grateful to be alive. I spent a week reflecting on my experience, talking with family and friends, hearing accounts of three people who had suddenly died of the same condition, and feeling more and more blessed to be amongst the living. I was beginning to change my perspective on life, and life was looking up. That is, until January 6, 2010.

I was hardly a full two weeks out of the hospital and I was experiencing excruciating pain in my abdomen. I've never had a child, but I imagine this is what contractions feel like: Intense pain, stop, intense pain, stop, and so on. The pain was so bad, I could barely talk. I was beginning to regurgitate, and with my grandmother standing over me, insisting I go to the emergency room, I resolved to go.

"Here we were again!" I thought. Blood work: Check! Results: normal. Examination: Check! Results: ruptured uterine fibroid, the size of a five-month-old fetus. Remedy: emergency myomectomy to remove the fibroid. Again, needless to say, I was dumbfounded and devastated.

I was facing not only weeks of hospitalization, but also a surgery that no surgeon wanted to take on because of the potential complications resulting from the pulmonary embolism. The doctors feared that due to the effects of Coumadin, the blood-thinner I was taking, I would bleed out during surgery. Yet, if they took me off the Coumadin to do the surgery, the blood clots could travel to my brain during or after surgery, causing death. It was a serious dilemma, and teams of doctors from several departments were working together to find a safe solution.

The next day, I was told that there was a surgeon who would perform the surgery, but for my safety, the doctors thought it best to implant an inferior vena cava filter to capture any traveling clots. I was also administered doses of Plasma, a blood thickener, and I was terrified! It was my first surgery, and such a risky one. "Lord, this is in your hands," I said. "Please keep me, I pray." And as I made this quick prayer, I was wheeled into surgery. A surgery I will not soon forget.

It lasted approximately eight hours, during which I began hemorrhaging, and was administered eight pints of blood. But, it wasn't the surgery that changed my life: it was the unexpected encounter I had the day after. That day, I saw "the Light."

Wait! Before you sigh in disbelief and close the book, let me just say that I know a few people may be skeptical, sarcastically thinking, "The Light? Really?" I know, because I used to be like them. Prior to this experience, I was also skeptical about "the Light." I've heard so many people talk about seeing "the Light" and frankly, I didn't believe them.

But, God obviously had something to prove, and now, I humbly admit that on Saturday, January 9, 2010, I saw the Light.

It was about eleven o'clock in the morning when the physician assistant entered my hospital room for her daily rounds. I was still very groggy from the anesthesia and just wanted to sleep. As she attended to me, I suddenly felt very dizzy and within a second or two of telling her so, I went unconscious. I flopped back on the bed with such force that it should have ripped open my freshly stapled incision. It is said that when one is passing away, hearing is the last thing to go. Well, the last thing I heard was the voice of the assistant screaming, "Stat!" Later on she said, "I knew something was really wrong when your eyes went blank, and even with the hospital's potent smelling salt, you would not wake up."

The next thing I saw was darkness, but that darkness quickly gave way to a bright light, and suddenly I was in the most beautiful place. To my left was a white wall, with beautiful red roses at its base, sloping upward toward the most radiant Light one could ever see. I felt like a child again. The Light shone so brightly that I could not look directly into it, but it was as if every ray was packed with immense love and peace. Immediately I was overcome by an indescribable sense of peace and love. This was a kind of love I had never felt before: It pierced my heart. It was deep, pure, resounding. This was true, real love. This was the kind of peace that I had never experienced before: It rested in my soul, serene. It was sweet peace. As I stood there, I inadvertently said, without fear, "Jesus." I said "Jesus" three times, and on the third I regained consciousness. The medical team was scurrying about, checking my heart and vital signs, but as I opened my eyes the name "Jesus" flowed from my lips. Thereafter, my life would not be the same.

I kept quiet about my encounter with the Light for a little while. I told my family and close friends, but I needed to process everything that had taken place up until that point. I began to do some self-evaluation: "If I die today, what will I have left? Who will I have been a blessing to? What has been the purpose of my life?" I knew my life had a purpose, a far greater one than I could have imagined. Otherwise the anemia would have killed me, the pulmonary embolism would have killed me, or the surgery would have killed me. So, I knew God had a purpose for me, but what was it? That's when I began to pray, "Lord, I want to live a purposeful life. I don't want to just live to live and die with no purpose. I want to know that I made a difference while I was here on earth. I want to know that I helped someone, blessed someone, and brought joy to someone. Lord, show me what *you* want me to do."

I spent roughly two weeks in the hospital recovering from surgery and working to get my Coumadin level where it needed to be for a safe discharge. When I was finally back at home, I was able to really reflect on my life. As I gradually healed, I began to feel the old "girl with a plan" Taneki coming back to life. I wanted to resume my life—yes, I would have a much different perspective, but I wanted to get back to my life and feel normal again.

It was now May 2010, and I was feeling excited about the spring and summer seasons. Granted, I was not all the way recovered. I was still on Coumadin and my body was still sensitive from surgery but, I was alive! Thank you, Lord! With great enthusiasm I began making plans, setting goals, and envisioning success. Little did I know, my darkest days were still ahead.

Pain began again, excruciating pain. On a scale of one to ten, this was fifty! "Lord, are you serious?" I thought. "This cannot happen again. I've had enough!" Now, I've always been one to handle pain well. I've always said, "If you don't think about it, you won't feel it." But not in this case! This pain was worse than the pain caused by the ruptured fibroid. This pain was off the Richter scale, and it was all centered at my left pelvic area. Here we go again!

Another emergency room visit. But, this time I was placed in the trauma unit. "I can't bear this!" I thought. It felt like my heart was about to stop at any moment from the pain, and now my legs were going numb. It was as if there was a huge silicone wrap on each leg, and the slightest touch sent pins and needles throughout my legs. I was crying like I'd never cried before. "I can't take this anymore!" I screamed. I couldn't lie back on the bed because the pain in my pelvis was too excruciating. I couldn't sit up because my legs were numb and it was all too painful. My mother held me up on my right, my aunt held me up on my left, and my dear grandmother was screaming, "She's going to die and no one is coming to help!"

I had no idea what was happening at this point. I was mentally drained, delirious from the pain. Finally, the head of the department came in, acknowledged that I was in severe pain, and administered morphine. But the morphine did nothing except made me nauseous. The doctor said, "Okay, so that didn't help. I'm going to give you a medication we use for pure pain. It's a non-narcotic and only used when pain is severe." That sounded more like it. "Bring it on!" I thought. But, this medication for "pure pain" did nothing to relieve me of mine.

It was now time for a CAT scan, but I still could not lie back on the bed. Despite the technician's plea that I try, there was no way I would be able to bear the pain. As she went to call the doctor, I sat there rocking back and forth and with tears streaming down my cheeks I prayed, "Lord, I trust you. Lord, please take this pain away from me. Lord, I need you. Lord, please take this away. Lord, please." That's all I could do. I had nothing else but prayer. All I could do was reach out to God. Just then, the doctor entered the room and administered another dose of morphine directly into my IV. Immediately the pain was gone, and it never returned.

Now I know, without a doubt, unequivocally, that this was not the work of the morphine, because it did not help me before. Nor was it the work of the non-narcotic, because that failed miserably. This was the work of God. Painkillers are a temporary fix and oftentimes require re-administration, but when God removes pain, He removes it permanently.

The CAT scan revealed that the IVC filter that was placed

in my vena cava prior to my surgery, had somehow turned, and the tiny prongs were poking through the vena cava, touching the aorta, which then bled into my pelvic area, causing a large hematoma, which rested on the nerves of my legs, causing the numbing—a mouthful, I know!

I spent four or five days in the hospital, three of which were spent in the ICU. In the end, with the fear of undertaking a risky surgery to retrieve the filter, the doctors decided to leave everything as is, hoping that scarring tissues would hold the IVC filter in its current position. And, it was after this last hospitalization that God truly had my full attention.

At this point, I had had just about enough of hospitals, and I fell into a deep depression, of which I could not see my way out. I felt like my life was in ruins. I didn't know if I was coming or going. "What happened to the Taneki that I'd known?" I thought. "What happened to my dreams, goals, and aspirations? What happened to my body and my energy? What happened to my life?" One minute I was perfectly healthy, and had never spent a day in the hospital in my life. The next minute I was being hospitalized for extensive periods of time, on a regular basis. I thought, "What went wrong, and how did this happen to me?" I was now limping on account of the nerve being pressed upon by the hematoma, still battling a fever of 103 degrees, and refusing to be hospitalized again. I was frankly, a hot mess—downtrodden, tired, and defeated. I was sinking into a black hole and I was sinking fast. I needed a way out. Then God, once again the God I loved but did not want to commit to, saw my needs and stepped in right on time.

Specks of light began to penetrate my darkness on May 8, 2010, when by the grace of God, my mother felt inclined to reach out to an old school friend, who also happened to be an ordained minister. As soon as my mother contacted her, led by the Spirit, she canceled all her appointments for the day and visited me. That day, she prayed and anointed me with oil, as James 5:14 instructs: "Is any one of you sick? He should call the elders of the church to pray over him and anoint him with oil in the name of the Lord." And this marked the inauguration of a new era, a new season in my life.

SPIRITUAL JOURNEY

Thanks to the grace of God, I immediately began feeling better and embarked on a spiritual journey. I knew I needed to make some radical changes in my life. Everything was different now. How I viewed life was completely different from how I viewed it before, and I was now spiritually and mentally ready to make the necessary changes.

I began what I call a "spiritual cleanse", which included a physical house cleaning (thoroughly cleaning out the clutter, getting rid of the old stuff), and a soul cleanse—confronting and letting go of past pains and disappointments. I began the process of forgiveness—of forgiving all whom I perceived to have done me wrong. Forgive my biological father: Check! Forgive my ex-boyfriend: Check! Forgive past friends who betrayed me: Check! Forgive, forgive, forgive: Check!

I needed to get rid of all the junk in my life in order to make space for God to come in and work. I saw what He did for me. I saw firsthand His love and grace working in my life, and I wanted more of Him. I spent time getting spiritually grounded: reading my bible, seeking the character of God, seeking wisdom, seeking knowledge, and most importantly, seeking understanding.

I didn't answer calls from friends and even gave up tickets to a concert that I would have cut an arm off for prior to this journey. I began seeing things for what they truly were and acknowledged that not everyone would be on this journey with me. Ties with some friends just needed to be broken. I prayed, worshiped, and fell in love with Jesus Christ. The specks of light became wider and wider each passing day, until I was suddenly standing in the complete fullness of His Light.

Although the journey may have been rough, painful, and scary at times, I wouldn't change my experiences for anything. I give God all the glory, honor, and praise. He kept me, even when I didn't know I needed to be kept. Each hospitalization brought me closer and closer to Jesus. And soon enough He didn't have to try, I was His and I've been His ever since.

In the process, I discovered that life, with all its glitz and glamour, means nothing without God. Frankly, if I'd known that a life "belonging to Christ"—otherwise known as a Christianity—would be filled with so much joy, peace, love, and victory, I would have dropped all "my plans" and signed up for His plans a long time ago. Everything I held on to, everything the world has to offer, cannot compare with having an intimate relationship with God.

On my journey, I discovered that all my misconceptions about Christianity were based on "religion" and the "religious," who, unfortunately, have been at the forefront of Christianity. I discovered that what God truly desires is intimacy—an intimate relationship, a friendship, a bond. I discovered that adhering to man-made rules and rituals did not impress Him—all He wanted was my heart.

MOVING FORWARD

Today my life can be summed up by Matthew 16:25: "For whoever desires to save his life will lose it, but whoever loses his life for My sake will find it." I gave up my desire to save my "life" and in return found life—abundance, blessings beyond measure, and real, unexpected victories.

Now, here are a few questions for you: Does God have your heart? Wait—before you quickly answer, take some time to think about it. Are you committed to Him, not only by words but by deeds? Having one foot in the world and another in the Kingdom does not equal commitment. To be committed, you must surrender your life in exchange for a new life in Christ. Are you saved? Meaning, have you received in your heart and confessed with your mouth Christ as your Lord and Savior? If you pass away today, are you sure of where you would spend eternity? Are you sure you would see the face of God? Can God trust you with the Kingdom blessings and Kingdom victories—will you give Him all the glory or will you keep some back for yourself? I know these are not easy questions. They require self-evaluation, but without self-evaluation there can be no growth, and without growth there can be no victories.

Pocket Full of Victories is based on my personal experiences, my journey to becoming a better person, a believer in Christ and living a life filled with victories. It is a real, fresh, and sometimes humorous look at what it took for me to leave the world's way behind and choose a life centered on my relationship with Jesus Christ.

I pray that everyone who reads this book will relate to it in some way, and be blessed by it in many ways. It was written for the unsaved—the I-want-to-believe-but-I'm-still-not-sure soon-to-be-believers, to inspire them to seek a new, victorious life in Christ. It was also written for the saved—new believers, young believers, and even matured believers—to motivate and encourage them to continue their journey in Christ and live victoriously.

If you fall into the category of "saved," you may proceed to Pocket One and continue on to the subsequent pockets. I've incorporated more information about my journey there, as well as provide invaluable information that I truly believe will be a blessing to you as you continue your victorious walk through Christ Jesus. Explore each pocket, carefully reading and meditating on the information provided. I've also provided areas after each pocket for you to write your thoughts and revelations as the Holy Spirit speaks to you. It is important to note that it does not matter how long you have been saved. Whether you were saved yesterday, or ten years ago makes no difference. Spiritual maturity is not dictated by the number of years saved, but by the ability to comprehend biblical principles, and effectively apply such principles to your life in order to live victoriously in Jesus Christ.

If, on the other hand, you are not sure about your salvation; you may fall into the category of the "unsaved." You may have not yet received Christ as your Lord and Savior but you are still seeking Him. You may feel lost and you're trying to find your way. You may have had an experience similar to mine but can't find the gratitude or joy for all that you've been through. Or, you may feel like there has to be more to life than what you've experienced; there may be a void in your life that you are trying to fill. Or, you may simply have a desire for more, more of God. If any of these situations sounds like your situation, **move on to Part B, "On the Fence."** There, I shed some light on some of the mysteries of biblical spirituality and address some of the concerns that keep us from forming an intimate relationship with God. At the end of it all, my hope is that I would have provided an opportunity for you to discover a new life in Christ, a life that's filled with the abundance of victories each and every day. God bless!

PART B

ON THE FENCE

(Myths, Mysteries and Misconceptions that keep us from God)

The lifestyle of a "Christian" never appealed to me. I wanted the "good life," with all the success to go along with it, and Christianity just did not fit into that picture. Sure, I wanted the happiness, the love, the peace, but I mainly wanted the fabulous life with all the fabulous trimmings. In my mind, Christianity was not that!

> I DIDN'T WANT ANY PART OF "RELIGION." IT WAS TOO COMPLICATED, I HAD FLAWS, I WOULDN'T BE ABLE TO LIVE UP TO THE STANDARDS, I'M TOO YOUNG, I STILL HAVE SOME PARTYING LEFT TO DO.

Christianity only represented all the "good" things I would have to give up. Everything about it just seemed restrictive, and I desired no part in it whatsoever. I just wanted to go to church from time to time, do my little "hallelujah" praise here and there, and no more! I really didn't feel the need to commit. After all, "my praise was as good as the next man's," I thought, "and God knows my heart."

I loved God and He conveniently fitted my lifestyle. But the thought of giving up my "life," all that I had known, all the "fun" things, to follow Christ was not an attractive thought. In fact, the thought scared me out of my wits! I just wanted to live my life without the complications of "religion." I didn't want to feel obligated to read the bible, which was a complete mystery to me. It was bad enough that I had no idea what it was saying: "Thou hath not; seethe thy; lest ye; oh thou"—really? And, to make things worse, I could hardly get through the first line without wanting to fall asleep. Yeah, that was not happening.

When I thought of "Christians," I didn't think of the old cliché: "Hypocrites." Instead, I thought of "no makeup," "long skirts," and "no dating." Plus, all they did was go to church! Everything, every area and activity in their life, seemed to be centered on church. No, that definitely was not appealing. But, for some reason, it seemed that God would always put these Christians in my life.

While I was in college, it felt like I was constantly being approached by a group of Christian college students bent on "saving" me. I was constantly being asked to attend bible study, and while I obliged a few times, I just could not see myself going every Friday night. After all, I had a "life" and "better" things to do. Nonetheless, all throughout my life, it seemed that God kept sending me little messages here and there. I felt that there was always a spiritual tug-of-war going on inside. God would push, and I would pull away. I tried running away from God so many times. It was simply hilarious—I was the Jonah of the 21st century.

The fact was, I didn't want any part of "religion." It was too complicated, I had flaws, I wouldn't be able to live up to the standards, I'm too young, I still have some partying left to do. I had so many excuses, but I just could not shake His hold on me.

I began to notice that at every turn, when it appeared that I was doing my own thing, living "life" on my terms, God would always be there to meet me. It seemed that He would always strategically place one of His saints directly in my path to speak with me, to encourage me, to step into my life when I needed it most. But, while I recognized His goodness, the idea of becoming a "Christian" still scared me. So, I resisted, I rebelled, and I rejected. I was "spiritual." I believed in God, I was familiar with Jesus, and that was good enough for me.

This tug-of-war went on until eventually, after all I went through, I surrendered. White flag waving, I gave up on a life that was riddled with ups and downs but very few lasting victories. In doing so, I discovered a life filled with unspeakable joy, indescribable peace, unfathomable love, and lasting, surpassing victories in Christ Jesus. Since then, I have never looked back. Sure, I'm still the same "girl with a plan," but now my plans are aligned with God's plans, and all I can see are the victories that lie ahead.

> THIS WALK DOES NOT REQUIRE THAT YOU ADHERE TO MAN-MADE RULES OR RITUALS. ON THIS JOURNEY, YOU'LL BE INTRODUCED TO GOD'S GRACE—HIS LOVE AND FAVOR WHEN YOU LEAST DESERVE IT, WHEN YOU HAVE DONE NOTHING TO EARN IT.

There are so many of you who may share the same sentiments about Christianity as I did. We've been plagued by images of Christian leaders who have fallen from grace. You may have been hurt by a few Christians right there in church. You may be confused about how to live for Christ. For various reasons, you may be on the fence, not sure if you want to make the commitment. You may even feel that "it does not take all of that," that just being a "good" person will get you through the pearly white gates of heaven. You may be confused about your relationship with God, Jesus, and the Holy Spirit. You may be turned off by those you've perceived to be "hypocrites," "bigots," or "holy rollers." Or, you just may not know. Whatever your reasons for not choosing a life in Christ, know that God loves you anyway, and all He desires is the love that lies in your heart.

Your commitment to God should not be contingent upon eternal circumstances or people. No, this is a personal, intimate walk with God. This is not about the Christian that hurt you, or the "hypocrites" in church, or the pastor whose secret life was just uncovered. This is simply about you and God. No one else matters in this equation.

This walk does not require that you adhere to man-made rules or rituals. On this journey, you'll be introduced to God's grace—His love and favor when you least deserve it, when you have done nothing to earn it. He'll give you his abounding grace so that you "may have the power to understand, as all God's people should, how wide, how long, how high, and how deep His love is. That you may experience the love of Christ, though it is too great to understand fully" (Ephesians 3:18-19 NLT). This walk is an invitation to victory, and the only guests invited are you and God. How will you respond?

The remainder of this section addresses some of the major reasons we hesitate to give ourselves over to Christ and hopefully clears up a few foggy areas. My prayer is that after you have read the additional information, you will have a new outlook on Christianity and will run towards Christ with the understanding that He does not require perfection. His arms are wide open to the willing heart.

Understanding the Godhead

Life is hectic, isn't it? We play so many roles. We are pulled in so many directions. We are but one human being wearing many different hats. We are known as parents to our children, wives and husbands to our spouses, employees to our bosses, friends to our friends, and so much more. Well, just as we are ONE being with many different titles, roles, and responsibilities, there is ONE God with three distinct persons and roles. There is God the Father, God the Son, and God the Holy Spirit. This is often referred to as the Holy Trinity or the Godhead.

> GOD IS NOT MAN, AND WE MUST NOT ASSIGN MANKIND'S LIMITATIONS TO HIM

Many people find this concept extremely hard to grasp. I've often heard people ask, "Well, how can ONE God be three different persons?" My response is, "Stop thinking of God in terms of what's possible for man!" We find it hard to comprehend that one God can be three distinct persons because we can't "intelligently" or "logically" see in our mind's eye how it is at all possible—that is, how it is at all "humanly" possible.

But, God is not human. He is the Creator of all things. He is omnipresent, omnipotent, omniscient—the one supreme, inexplicable God, who is to be feared, revered, loved, obeyed, and looked at in wonderment and awe.

Think about this: If we believe that God exists, that He created the heavens and the earth, the sky, the trees, the wind, the sea, the air, all things, then why does it seem so impossible that He—all-powerful, all-knowing, almighty God—could be God the Father, God the Son, and God the Holy Spirit? God is not man, and we must not assign mankind's limitations to Him. As much as we would love to, we are not able to clone ourselves into three distinct persons. It is humanly impossible for us to function one hundred percent as an employee, a parent, and a spouse all at the same time, but for God, nothing is impossible.

God the Father is creator of all things. Through Him all things are and apart from Him nothing is. He had the vision for the heavens and the earth. He had the vision for all living things, spoke it all into existence, formed man from dust in His own image and blew breath into man. He is the giver of all things good. He gave us the gift of eternal life through His Son, Jesus Christ. It is because of this gift that we are now children of God and able to refer to Him as Abba, Father.

Jesus is the Son of God—God's only begotten, his unique Son. He is the Bread of Life (John 6:35) and the giver of life. He sustains and nourishes the souls of the believers. He is the Light of the world (John 8:12), the one and only true Light that's able to penetrate and devour the deepest darkness. He is the Door for the sheep (John 10:7). It is through Him we enter into the Kingdom of Heaven. He is the Good Shepherd (John 10:11), the one who leads us, protects us, feeds us, takes care of all of our needs, guides us, and never allows us to stray too far from Him. He is the Resurrection and the Life (John 11:25). It is through our faith in Him that our old lives die and a new life, a new spiritual life is resurrected. He is the Way, the Truth, and the Life (John 14:16). He is the only true path to God, and the only means to eternal life. He is the True Vine (John 15:1). It is through our attachment to Him that we are able to bear fruit, to produce the visible spiritual and physical evidence of our new lives in Him.

He is the God of salvation, the great "I AM," our savior, redeemer, deliverer, healer, and the mediator between us and the Father. Through Him our sins are forgiven. Through Him and His shed blood on the cross, we have been given bold access to the throne of God. The shedding of His blood was ransom for our lives, and through faith in Jesus Christ we are sanctified, set apart, set free, justified (declared not guilty, freed from the guilt of our past) and declared righteous. Through Christ, we have life and life more abundantly.

The Holy Spirit is the third person of the Holy Trinity. He is the Spirit of Christ that lives in believers, who never leaves or forsakes us. The Holy Spirit is the promise of God to the believer, the Spirit of Truth, leading us in all things true. He is the Helper, the Advocate, and the Comforter. His role is to lead us, guide us, teach us and reveal truths to us—alerting our senses the truth. He intercedes on our behalf, convict us of our misdeeds, imparts spiritual gifts, and molds us into the persons—the children, servants, and disciples—that the Father has called us to be. He bestows wisdom, knowledge, and understanding. He gives clarity to scriptures and brings them to our remembrance. He pours into our hearts the love of God, empowers us to share the Gospel of Jesus Christ, and functions as a supernatural enabler, enabling us to walk upright. He is the supernatural on our natural, empowering us to accomplish all that the Father has called us to do.

One God, three distinct divine entities all working together for the well-being of humanity, all working together as ONE whole unit to give us an immeasurable life of victories.

Blanket Spirituality

"I'm spiritual." "I believe in the universe, and I give thanks to nature." "These are modern times and I believe in new-age spirituality." Have you heard any of these statements before? I have! They came right from my mouth—at least the "I'm spiritual" statement did. I was one of the "spiritual" folks who had no desire to be labeled. I was an educated, open-minded intellectual, who refused to be placed in a religious box. I was "cool."

One of the things I would pray for was for God to put "spiritually grounded" people in my life. Then, one day I started noticing that the people I was attracting were spiritual, all right. They were spiritually confused! Notwithstanding,

I embraced this "spiritual" ideology up until the point of what I call my "brokenness," the point when I knew I needed God and needed to know more about Him. As I began my spiritual quest to know my Lord, I thought, "What does it mean to be truly spiritual, and what is the basis of my spirituality?"

> THE UNIVERSE, THE EARTH, NATURE—ALL THESE "THINGS" TO WHICH WE GIVE PRAISE —WOULD NOT EXIST IF IT WERE NOT FOR GOD.

There are so many of us walking around referring to ourselves as "spiritual," not wanting to call the name of Jesus or associate our spirituality with any "religious" beliefs. We refer to God as the "universe," take "Christ" out of "Christmas," and give thanks to "nature," the "sun," the "moon," and everything in between. We do all this while ignoring the fact that the universe, the earth, nature—all these "things" to which we give praise—would not exist if it were not for God.

Now, I respect everyone's religious beliefs. But the truth is that giving thanks and praise to "things" without acknowledging the Creator is not only idolatrous but it is an offense to God. Nothing exists apart from God.

At this point, let me say this: There is nothing essentially wrong with being "spiritual." In fact, I still consider myself "spiritual" as opposed to "religious." But the basis of my spirituality is now in core relation to my relationship with my Lord and Savior, Jesus Christ. The foundation of my spirituality is now God and God alone.

Forget everything you thought you knew about Christianity. Forget all you thought it was. Forget the stigma and stereotypes related to Christians. Know that at the end of the day and at the core of it all, it simply means "belonging to Christ." It simply means you are a child of God, adopted by faith in Jesus Christ. Jesus is "the way, the truth and the life. No one comes to the Father except through Him" (John 14:6). While other religions point to some divine truth—some divine savior, Christianity is the only religion that has a religious figure proclaiming divine deity with the historical evidence to prove it.

This world has so many different religions and different beliefs. It seems as if every day there are new religions being formed by people who claim to have received divine revelation. As a society, we are seeking, searching, looking for some place to belong, something higher than ourselves to believe in. But we must move away from blanket spirituality, which is only a façade, concealing the depth of our ignorance about our Creator.

Jesus said, "Whoever denies Me before men, him I will also deny before My Father who is in heaven" (Matthew 10:33). We must boldly acknowledge Christ at all times and in every area of our lives. Life is meaningless apart from God. There is nothing that is able to give us what God is able to give us—not nature, not the universe, not plants, not animals, not carved images. There is nothing that is able to give us the love, joy, peace, and life that Christ offers to those who believe.

Choosing to move away from the ambiguity of "spirituality" and clearly defining myself as one saved, redeemed, and set free by Jesus Christ has enabled me to develop an intimate relationship with my heavenly Father. Knowing Him intimately has led me to countless victories, and the same is possible for you. We are all God's creation, but until we receive Christ as Lord and Savior, we are *not* all His children. So I encourage you to become a child of God today. Victory awaits!

I'M A GOOD PERSON—I'M DEFINITELY GOING TO HEAVEN, RIGHT?

Sorry to burst your bubble but...wrong! If you were to hit the streets with a survey in your hand, asking people why they believed they were going to heaven, the number one response would most likely be, "because I am a good person." Oftentimes we think that our good deeds and loving kindness are the golden tickets, guaranteeing us an entrance into the gates of heaven. But, let's take some time to examine this assumption.

> IF WE GOT THROUGH THE PEARLY GATES BASED ON OUR "GOOD DEEDS," HEAVEN WOULD BE WORSE THAN A MODERN-DAY REALITY SHOW—DRAMA, DRAMA, AND MORE DRAMA!

Imagine that our "good works" got us into heaven. If you can imagine that, then imagine heaven being filled with big "holy" egos everywhere! I can see it now: There would be debates and discussions all over heaven about who did what and for whom. There would be arguments about who did more for humanity, who gave more, who fed more, who saved the planet, who deserved to be there and who didn't.

I imagine Henry, chest high, nose pointed in the air, boasting, "I saved the poor people of Asia with my nonprofit organization." And then Steven, trying to get one up on Henry, boasting, "Well, I saved Africa *and* the Caribbean by providing clean water to the poor." And then Elena—oh no, Elena will not be outdone by Steven or Henry—boasts, "I saved the lives of women and their families all over the world by providing them with grants to start their own businesses." Can you imagine it? Heaven would be filled with huge Wall Street–type egomaniacs, all arguing about which crown of glory they should get. All bragging about what they did to make it into heaven, requesting to see management because "the big Man must have gotten it wrong! After all, I gave millions, and Jonathan only gave a few bucks to the homeless man at the end of his block. There is no way we should be in the same place!" I tell you, if we got through the pearly gates based on our "good deeds," heaven would be worse than a modern-day reality show—drama, drama, and more drama!

Heaven by deeds would be like high school all over again. There would be the "cool" clique of people who, while on earth, had the multi-million dollar philanthropy budgets; the "nerds," who gave what they could with limited budgets; the "losers," who gave what they had, if and when they had it; and the "jocks," a subsection of the cool clique, who dedicated themselves to saving the planet. There would be cliques within cliques and chaos upon chaos, and many of us would be looking for a quick transfer to anywhere *but* heaven!

Now, here's another thought: If we all got into heaven because we are "good people," then what was the purpose of Jesus and what use would He be to us today? This question requires serious thought. Too many of us believe that we can "work" our way into heaven, when in fact, the only way to get into heaven is to receive Christ as your Lord and Savior. That's it!

Your works will *not* get you in. Your charming personality will *not* get you in. Your good heart will *not* get you in. The fact that you embraced world peace and sang "Kumbaya" while holding hands with people of other races will *not* get you in. Regardless of what you think, not one person is made righteous by "good" deeds. We are all sinners: "for all have sinned and fall short of the glory of God and a man is justified and made upright by faith, independent of and distinctly apart from good deeds" (Romans 3:23; 28). "God saves us by his grace when we believe, and we can't take credit for this; it is a gift from God. Salvation is not a reward for the good things we have done, so none of us can boast about it" (Ephesians 2:8-9). The one and only way into the Kingdom of heaven is through faith in Jesus Christ.

"For God so loved the world that He gave His only begotten Son, that whoever believes in Him should not perish but have everlasting life. For God did not send His son into the world to condemn the world, but that the world through Him might be saved" (John 3:16-17). This is the agape love that

God has for us—that unselfish, undeserving, ever-abundant, ever-flowing, incomprehensible love—that through His grace, provides us with a way out of our messes. Jesus paid the price when He died on the cross for our sins. He died so that through Him, we may be saved—receive eternal life and become citizens of the Kingdom of heaven.

So, to all who feverishly toil, hoping, believing that it is the key into the pearly white gates of heaven, Jesus says: "Come to Me, all you who labor and are heavy laden, and I will give you rest" (Matthew 11:25). Salvation is not by your works. The one and only way to be saved, to receive eternal life and see the wonderful, glorious heavens is to receive God's free gift of salvation through faith: Confess with your mouth, believe and receive in your heart the Son of God, Jesus Christ, as your Lord and Savior (Roman 10:9). The choice is yours: work in vain or receive your free gift to bountiful victories. The choice is yours. My prayer is that you choose victory through Jesus today!

I've Made Some Mistakes—I'm Not Worthy.

First and foremost, who hasn't? Mistakes or not, you are worthy! Yes, you—you are worthy! You with your head hanging low, feeling sorry for yourself—you are worthy! You who have betrayed others—you are worthy! You murderer, you thief, you liar, you cheat—you are worthy! You with that secret addiction—you are worthy! You who have been abused and misused—you are worthy! You who came from the other side of the tracks—you are worthy! You with the spirit of jealousy and envy—you are worthy! You backbiter, you backslider—you are worthy! You, you, and you—you are worthy! God loves you so much, despite your past. No matter who you are, what you have done, or what you have been through, God says you are worthy!

> GOD LOVES YOU AND THERE IS NOTHING IN THE WORLD—NO CRUDE ACT, NO ACT OF BETRAYAL, NOTHING THAT YOU HAVE DONE OR THAT HAS BEEN DONE TO YOU—THAT WOULD MAKE GOD SAY YOU'RE NOT WORTHY OF HIS LOVE. YOU ARE WORTHY. YOU ALWAYS HAVE BEEN, AND YOU WILL ALWAYS BE WORTHY

There is nothing that you have done that God will not forgive. He is chasing after you with the gift of forgiveness. When you seek Him and have a heart of repentance, there are no mistakes, no bad deeds, nothing bad enough for God to turn His back on you. You are worthy to be saved and worthy of His grace and love. It does not matter how things look to you or how you are feeling. God loves you and there is nothing in the world—no crude act, no act of betrayal, nothing that you have done or that has been done to you—that would make God say you're not worthy of His love. You are worthy. You always have been, and you will always be worthy.

So often we want more of God. We want to be drawn closer to Him, but our past holds us back. Our past failures, deeds, and mistakes are constant reminders of a life we so desperately want to forget. It is a daunting memorial which leaves us feeling less than, worthless, and in despair. We often think that we are not good enough, or not perfect enough, but here's a little tip for you: God does not care about your flaws, your shortcomings, your past mistakes or sins. He simply wants you to come as is—with flaws, faults and all.

God is in the business of restoration and restitution. Everything that was taken from you, every dream derailed, innocence lost, every future stolen, God is faithful to restore. Not only that, He will give you double for all the troubles of your past (Zechariah 9:12). When you seek Him with all your heart, mind, and soul, He is faithful to give you "beauty for ashes." God will restore the beauty of everything in you that has been devoured by the fires of life. For all the years you've mourned your past, all your secret tears, God is faithful to give you "the oil of joy." For everything that's been weighing you down, all the heaviness of your heart and spirit, God is faithful to clothe you in "the garment of praise" (Isaiah 61:3).

It is the trick of the enemy (yes, the devil is real) to make us believe that God would never want us because of our past. It's his trick to have us "feel" and believe that we have nothing to offer and that God could never use us for anything good. But the devil is a liar (John 8:44), for "God has chosen the foolish things of the world to put to shame the wise, and God has chosen the weak things of the world to put to shame the things which are mighty; and the base things of the world and the things which are despised God has chosen, and the things which are not, to bring to nothing the things that are" (1 Corinthians 1:27-28).

So, believe me when I tell you that you—with your checkered past—are exactly who God uses to uplift His Kingdom. And, when you begin to seek Him with your heart, when you begin to confess your sins and have a heart of repentance, "He is faithful and just to forgive you your sins, and to cleanse you from all unrighteousness" (1 John 1:9). When you seek Him, receive Him, and confess the errors of your ways, He promises to blot out your transgressions and never to remember your sins (Isaiah 43:25). That's the God we serve! He is not like man—He will not dangle your past over your head as a daily reminder of every wrongful thought, deed, or act. In fact, He says, "Do not remember the former things, nor consider the things of old. Behold, I will do a new thing" (Isaiah 43:18-19). God is ready, able, and willing to forgive you, cleanse you, set you free—He is ready to make you brand new.

> GOD IS IN THE BUSINESS OF RESTORATION AND RESTITUTION. EVERYTHING THAT WAS TAKEN FROM YOU, EVERY DREAM DERAILED, INNOCENCE LOST, EVERY FUTURE STOLEN, GOD IS FAITHFUL TO RESTORE.

What the enemy meant for evil, God shall make for your good (Genesis 5:20). Know today, believe today that you are worthy of His love and forgiveness. A change can take place right now. Everything in your past that has been holding you back from a closer relationship with your heavenly Father can be removed from your life today, if you allow Him in. Seek Him, confess your sins, ask for forgiveness, and as you do so, have faith that you are forgiven. Forgive yourself as He has forgiven you, and enter into a new relationship with your Lord and Savior Jesus Christ. You are worthy of every victory God has in store for you. Receive Christ today because you are worthy!

I'm Not Sure—What If I Mess Up?

So, what *if* you mess up? The world is not going to end, believe me. And here's a little secret: No one is perfect. Yes, that's it! No one is perfect, so stop worrying about messing up!

I know, I know—there are a lot of people out there who would like to give the impression that they are perfect. They are quick to belittle ("I can't believe he had the nerve to show his face in church!"), quick to judge ("I can tell she is a heathen. Look at her dress!"), quick to turn up their noses ("I'm sorry, but you can't sit here!"). But, despite the façade, despite their perfect attendance record in church, despite their fasting twice per week and praying all day long, despite their "holier than thou" attitudes, they are in no way perfect. In fact, behind closed doors, these seemingly perfect individuals may be the most flawed of all.

> WE THINK WE HAVE TO BE PERFECT, FLAWLESS, AND COMPLETELY DISCIPLINED TO LIVE FOR GOD.

Now, I know I may have ruffled a few feathers or raised a few eyebrows. But, please understand that while I am in no way justifying sin, the reality is that like all of us, you will "mess up," and from time to time, you will "fall short of the glory of God" (Romans 3:23). The good news is that it is all a part of the spiritual-growth process. It is our ability, along this journey, to learn from our shortcomings that determines our level of spiritual maturity. It is through this learning process that we gracefully develop from spiritual babes into spiritually matured Christians.

Know and believe that no man is error-proof—none, not one! Not Holy Ghost filled, speaking-in-tongues Sister Kathy, not Pastor So-and-So of the Living Christ Baptist Methodist Episcopal Pentecostal Evangelist Church of God AME, not "hallelujah"-shouting, jumping and praising Auntie Sue, not long-skirt-and-turtleneck-wearing Beth, not one man is perfect. The only perfect being to ever exist on the face of the earth was Jesus Christ.

"I know that nothing good lives in me, that is, in my sinful nature. I want to do what is right, but I can't. I want to do what is good, but I don't. I don't want to do what is wrong, but I do it anyway" (Romans 7:18-19 NLT). These are the words of Apostle Paul, one of the greatest and most transparent apostles. And yet, from these words we can see that he himself was not flawless or faultless. This was the great Apostle Paul! The first time I read this scripture, it blew my mind.

I was always so hard on myself. I was so afraid of messing up. And if I did slip up, I would feel such crippling guilt. I would spend my time feeling angry, disappointed with myself, and sad that I messed up. After all, why should I mess up? I was now a child of God, living for God, knowing the word of

God. There was no reason for any form of "non-Christian-like" behavior or thought. There was no reason for me to mess up—well, except for the fact that I am human. But, apart from that, there was no reason for me to mess up at all! Needless to say, I was and still am developing, but thank God for the epistles of Apostle Paul. This scripture really put things into perspective for me. I could now let go of the notion of perfection, and joyfully embrace the conviction of the Holy Spirit—allowing the Spirit of God to mold me, teach me, and lead me on the path of His righteousness.

> RELEASE YOURSELF FROM THE IDEOLOGY OF PERFECTION, WHICH IS NOTHING BUT A STRONGHOLD, A BARRIER HOLDING YOU BACK FROM THE TRUE JOY, PEACE, FULFILLMENT, RICHES, AND VICTORIES THAT COME FROM AN INTIMATE RELATIONSHIP WITH YOUR LORD AND SAVIOR.

We think we have to be perfect, flawless, and completely disciplined to live for God. But even Apostle Paul, with all the signs and wonders that followed him, was not perfect or sinless. Not one believer is perfect. We all mess up sometimes. Let's face it—it's not like we came from our mother's womb shouting "hallelujah!" We have been a part of the world and the world's system for a long time, and at the end of the day, we must recognize that change will not come overnight.

Think about it. If for 20 years or more you have been engaged in the same behaviors, had the same attitudes, same speech patterns, same thoughts, do you really think that you will be transformed into a saint overnight? No! We must "work out our own salvation" (Philippians 2:12), and this is the spiritual-growth process. Note: We do not work *for* our salvation, as that is a gift, but we do work *out* our own salvation; "for God is working in us, giving us the desires and the power to do what pleases him" (Philippians 2:13 NLT). This is a lifelong process, but thank God for the gift of the Holy Spirit who works within us to bring about spiritual change.

I implore you: Release yourself from the ideology of perfection, which is nothing but a stronghold, a barrier holding you back from the true joy, peace, fulfillment, riches, and victories that come from an intimate relationship with your Lord and Savior. If, while on this Christian journey, you "mess up," know that God does not condemn, as "there is no condemnation for those who belong to Christ Jesus" (Romans 8:1). Therefore, any crippling guilt you may feel after you've repented does not come from God, because He is faithful to forgive. God knew you were going to make your mistakes before *you* knew you were going to make them. He knows us better than we know ourselves.

Look at Peter. At the last supper he boldly proclaimed, "Lord, I am ready to go with You, both to prison and to death" (Luke 22:33). Yet at the very hour of Christ's betrayal, Peter denied knowing Jesus three times. Surely, he messed up! But regardless of all of Peter's mistakes, he still went on to become a great apostle of Christ, preaching the first sermon at Pentecost, with great signs and wonders following him.

God is full of grace and He sees the weaknesses in us that we don't see in ourselves. While it's not His will for us to fall, it is in the moments of "messing up" that we gain our testimonies and develop a deeper understanding of the nature and love of our Lord. When we mess up, we must simply repent (have a change of heart and mind), ask for forgiveness, and pray for God's grace to help us change the things in us that are not pleasing to Him. The reality is, there are just some things about ourselves that we can't change on our own. We don't have the strength to change certain habits or behaviors. But, when we call upon the grace of God to help us change, His supernatural power will enable us to do what we cannot do with our natural abilities.

> ONE OF THE BIGGEST MISCONCEPTIONS IS THAT WE HAVE TO "GET IT TOGETHER" BEFORE WE GIVE OURSELVES OVER TO THE LORD. WE THINK OF COMING TO CHRIST AS AN EVENT.

I encourage you to dismiss the thought of "messing up," accept that you are not and will never be perfect, and choose to enter into a deeper relationship with your Creator. As you begin your journey, trust in Him, ask for His grace, stay in His word, and soon enough you'll begin to bear the fruit of His righteousness. "He who has begun a good work in you will complete it" (Philippians 1:6). There is no perfect being, but there is a perfect and good God waiting for you to come to Him today.

Yes, but Let Me First Get Things in Order

You wake up in the morning, get dressed and make sure you are looking your best. You glance at yourself in the mirror and think, "Not bad. Looking good today." Hair: Check! Clothes: Check! Perfume: Check! Attitude: Check! Off for the day you go, looking good and feeling good. But, then you notice that you left your wallet at home—you have no money, no credit cards. You made sure everything was in order, but you forgot to put the one essential item in order. Well, that's how it is with our spiritual life. We work to put everything in order except the one essential thing necessary to live victoriously and to have eternal life.

Think about it. As we age, we try to put all our affairs in order. We make sure our wills are in order and that money is available to our loved ones, that our children are taken care of, that our spouses are taken care of, that our house is in order and our paperwork is in order. We make sure to have things in place to help and support our loved ones in the event of our demise. But so often, while making sure "everything" is in order, we neglect to get spiritually in order. We neglect to reconcile with God through His son, Jesus Christ.

One of the biggest misconceptions is that we have to "get it together" before we give ourselves over to the Lord. We think of coming to Christ as an event. We think, "Let me get the sin out of my life first, and then I'll come." It's an event and we are the organizers, promoters, and hosts. We have a mental list of things we believe we need to make happen first, like: Find a church, buy a new suit, buy some shoes, find the time to attend church on a regular basis, change myself, drop Mr. Wrong, drop Ms. Wrong, cut ties with those folks. And the list goes on and on.

We want more and we say, "Yes, *but...*" There is always a "but," and those "buts" make us second-guess ourselves and keep us from truly living victoriously. While we are busy with our "buts," I truly believe that God is saying, "Get your 'buts' out of the way and surrender your life to Me. Seek Me, choose Me first, and I will put your entire life in order." "Seek FIRST the kingdom of God and His righteousness, and all these things shall be added to you" (Matthew 6:33). Everything you need, everything you desire, is in God and God alone.

I, along with so many others, have thought, "I'm not ready yet. I want to make sure I'm ready." But here's another little secret for you: If you are waiting for the "perfect" time to commit to Christ, then, I'm sorry to inform you, there will never be one. We will never have "everything" in order all at the same time. That would make us superheroes and, frankly, I can't recall the last time I saw a flying cape in tights outside of my window. No, there is no perfection in time. And, at the risk of sounding like a "brimstone-and-fire Bible Belt street preacher," I must say that the grim, yet true reality is that tomorrow is promised to no man. Now, I know it's a cliché. You've heard it over and over again.

> ALL THAT'S NEEDED, ALL THAT'S NECESSARY RIGHT AT THIS VERY MOMENT IS A DEEP DESIRE FOR MORE.

But, my time spent in and out of the hospital has taught me that there is no time like the present to start a new life in Christ.

I have learned that surrendering to Christ is not a major production. You don't need to try on the costume to see if it fits, His glory perfectly fits. There is no need to check the lighting. His light never dims. There is no need for a sound check. He'll speak directly to your heart. The cast is simply you, the Father, the Son, and the Holy Spirit, and there is no need for a rehearsal. It's ad lib all the way.

> YOU NEED NOT WORRY ABOUT CHANGING YOURSELF, BECAUSE THE HOLY SPIRIT WILL MOLD YOU INTO THE PERSON YOU WERE MEANT TO BE, CHANGING YOUR VERY NATURE TO ONE IN SPIRITUAL UNION WITH GOD.

All that's needed, all that's necessary right at this very moment is a deep desire for more. A yearning for change, a need for deliverance from the dark and oppressive mental space you may be in, a yearning to be loved like you've never been loved before, a yearning to feel peace like you've never felt before, and a desire to feel joy like you've never felt before. All this is possible, and the only requirements are a willing heart of repentance, a surrendering spirit, and lips that cry out for Jesus to take residence in your heart and change your life. That's it—that's all it takes. Christ has already placed your victories in order, and all you need to do is put Him first.

OKAY, I WANT JESUS. SO WHAT HAPPENS NEXT?

The next step is to officially receive your free gift of salvation by receiving Christ as your Lord and Savior. In doing so, He will come into your heart through the Holy Spirit. When you have received the Holy Spirit, He will take residence in your heart and the regeneration process will begin.

Regeneration is the work of the Holy Spirit to give a new life to the believer. It is the cleansing and purification work of the Holy Spirit to bring about a spiritual change in the believer, transforming him or her from spiritual death to spiritual life. Therefore you need not worry about changing yourself, because the Holy Spirit will mold you into the person you were meant to be, changing your very nature to one in spiritual union with God.

> YOU WILL NOT RECEIVE SALVATION TONIGHT AND WAKE UP TOMORROW A PERFECT BEING.

It is important to note again that this spiritual change will not be done overnight. God is not a genie; this is not "rub my belly and give me three wishes, God." You will not receive salvation tonight and wake up tomorrow a perfect being. There is a spiritual-growth process that comes from "working out your own salvation" (Philippians 2:12). Spiritual development and growth are necessary and comes from a renewed mind. But the Spirit of God will always be there to empower you and lead you on the path of righteousness.

If you are genuinely in need of a change in your life—tired of the same cycles, the darkness, the pain—if you desire an intimate relationship with your Creator and want to have Christ in your life, please take a look at the Prayer for Salvation on the next page. Now, although I wrote it, I exhort you to make this prayer your prayer, make these words your words—let it flow directly from your heart. In doing so, Christ will meet you exactly where you are, and so will begin the start of a great new life, a great new adventure in Christ.

"If you confess with your mouth the Lord Jesus and believe in your heart that God has raised Him from the dead, you will be saved" (Romans 10:9). Victory awaits—invite Christ in today!

Moving On to the Subsequent Chapters

In the subsequent chapters, I have incorporated more information about my own journey and provided what I refer to as "pockets," containing invaluable information for living an abundant, victorious life in Christ Jesus.

Explore each pocket, carefully reading and meditating on the information. I've also provided areas after each pocket for you to write down your own revelations as the Holy Spirit speaks to you. My prayer is that as you effectively apply the information to your life, soon enough the person you used to be will cease to exist, and your life will burst open with new possibilities, new hopes, and new dreams. I decree victory is yours in Jesus's name! God bless you!

PRAYER FOR SALVATION

"Heavenly Father, I humbly come before you and confess that I have sinned. I confess that I have not been living a life pleasing to You. Father, forgive me of all my sins, sins I am aware of and sins I am not. I repent and turn my mind and my heart to You. I confess that I believe that Jesus is the son of God and that He died for my sins. I believe that He was resurrected and today He lives. Holy Spirit, come into my heart, take over my life. I surrender my heart, mind, and soul to you. Thank you Lord for saving me. In Jesus's name I pray. Amen."

Sign: _____ Date: _____

POCKET
1

ABBA'S CHILD

TANEKI DACRES 53

Congrats! You are a believer; you've received Christ as your Lord and Savior. Now it is time to live victoriously. But before we move on, let me ask you this: Do you know who you are? No, not your birth name! Do you know who you are now that you are a born-again believer?

One of the key principles to walking in victory is knowing who you are and whose you are, and understanding how that relationship impacts your life.

Now, let me start by saying that you are not who you used to be. I know your identification card contains your first, middle, and last names, but today you have a new identity in Christ. Today you are a child of God.

> DESPITE WHAT YOUR EARTHLY FATHER DID OR DIDN'T DO, YOUR HEAVENLY FATHER WILL NEVER DISAPPOINT YOU. HIS ARMS ARE ALWAYS OPEN, AND HE IS ALWAYS WILLING TO POUR HIS LOVE INTO YOUR LIFE.

If that did not come as a surprise to you, you may have thought that you were already a child of God, but the fact is, prior to being saved you were simply one of God's wonderful creations. Now, thanks to Jesus, you have been reborn and reconciled to the Father, adopted through faith as His child. John 1:12 tells us: "As many as received Him, to them He gave the right to become children of God, to those who believe in His name." Galatians 3:26 says: "For you are all sons of God through faith in Christ Jesus." When we receive Christ through faith, God adopts us as His children (Galatians 4:5).

As His children we "are no longer strangers and foreigners. We are citizens along with all of God's holy people. We are members of God's family" (Ephesians 2:19 NLT). Through this adoption, we are now "His chosen people, a royal priesthood—kings and priests set apart to offer spiritual sacrifices to God; a holy nation—sanctified for God's purpose; His own special people—protected and taken care of by God" (1Peter 2:5-9). Through this reconciliation, we, as His children, are given the honor and privilege to join Christ in calling the Creator "Abba, Father" (Romans 5:15).

The word "Abba" is the Aramaic word for "Father" or "My Father." It denotes a personal, intimate relationship with God and affirms our adoption into the family of God.

WHAT DOES IT MEAN TO BE A CHILD OF GOD?

So now you know for sure that you are a child of God, belonging to Christ. Great! But how does this revelation translate to a victorious life? How does this relationship impact your life?

Well, the fact that you are a child of God means several things. First, it means that unlike some earthly fathers, your heavenly Father will never leave you. Unlike some earthly fathers, your heavenly Father is always there for you. Unlike some earthly fathers, your heavenly Father will always provide for you. Unlike some earthly fathers, your heavenly Father loves you unconditionally.

Think of the characteristics of the best earthly father you

can possibly think of. It may be your biological father, a stepfather, a television character, a friend, or simply a figment of your imagination. Regardless of who it is, your heavenly Father has all his characteristics and so many more. He is supremely incomparable.

Abba, Father surpasses everything we could ever want in a Father. He is always there to comfort us, lead us, chastise us when we need a little chastisement. He is always dependable, always faithful, always filled with love and complete joy. This is what it means to be a child of God—it means that despite what your earthly father did or didn't do, your heavenly Father will never disappoint you. His arms are always open, and He is always willing to pour His love into your life.

> I NO LONGER SAW GOD AS THIS SUPERNATURAL ENTITY THAT I PRAYED TO FROM TIME TO TIME. HE WAS NOW TRULY ABBA, FATHER.

Knowing that we are children of God also gives us the confidence to go boldly to His throne—bringing boldly and without hesitation our cares, concerns, requests, and thoughts. It is through this confidence that we are able to see the visible manifestations of victory in our lives.

I remember the first time I had the revelation about my identity. It was such a "wow moment" and it left me absolutely speechless. It was one afternoon while watching a gospel service on television, that as I sat on the side of my bed, God spoke into my heart and said, "All these years, you've secretly wished that you had father who was there. All these years, you've wondered what it would have been like to be daddy's girl. And all this time, you have had Me." Needless to say, I was flabbergasted! Flooded with emotion, all I could do was just sit there, eyes wide open, heart beating fast, repeating over and over, "I have a Father, I have a Father! A Father who loves me unconditionally. A Father I can talk to, one to whom I can take all my concerns, issues, hurts—anything and everything. I have a Father who is there for me, one to lead and direct me. A Father who will never leave me, and is able to do greater things than any earthly father could ever do?!" It was a question, an answer, and a statement all at the same time. That moment completely changed my life and my walk with Christ. It was with that divine revelation that I no longer saw God as this supernatural entity that I prayed to from time to time. He was now truly Abba, Father, and it was on that foundation I built an intimate relationship with my Lord.

I Know Him...I Think

For so long I thought I knew God. "Come on, He's God!" I'd exclaim. "God is God. There's no explaining Him! He is just, you know, God!" Like many of you, I knew how to pray under fire, how to shout my "thank you, God!" in times of victory, and my "oh God, help me, please!" in times of need. I bought into "blanket spirituality" and "positive thoughts"—the whole "I" movement—yet still, I felt God and I were on "good terms." Buddies, even! But, did I really know Him?

Eventually, after I surrendered my life to Christ, I realized that, while being spiritual and thinking positively are great, if all I knew about God was the basic "Jesus wept"—if my foundation was not in God, and who I was to Him, then when faced with the realities, struggles, and disappointments of life, I was in for some serious trouble because what I thought I knew I didn't know. I did not know my heavenly Father.

What I've come to realize is that knowing my identity through Christ and truly knowing God are two of the major keys to victories. Events that threw me for a loop made it obvious to me that the God I thought I knew so well was not the anchor for my spirituality or positive thoughts. It became clear that I really didn't know Him at all. I was ignorant about who He was and who I was to Him, and therefore every "positive" effort I made before possessing this knowledge was like a ship sailing with a gaping hole. Eventually it sank.

Discovering who I was and whose I was marked the start of a brand-new life. But that revelation was just the beginning—I needed to dig a little deeper. Now that I had my heavenly identity down, my next thought was, "Okay, so I'm a child of God. But who really is God?" You may think that that was a strange question, but I needed to move beyond surface-level spirituality. This treasure I was seeking was in the depths of the deep, and a spiritual excavation was needed. I was seeking, search-

> I NEEDED TO MOVE BEYOND SURFACE-LEVEL SPIRITUALITY. THIS TREASURE I WAS SEEKING WAS IN THE DEPTHS OF THE DEEP, AND A SPIRITUAL EXCAVATION WAS NEEDED.

ing to know Him intimately.

QUEST FOR INTIMACY

I needed to know more about my heavenly Father. I needed to know more about Him because I was falling in love with Him. I needed to know more because even when I chose the world over Him, He kept His hands on me, never leaving me alone. I needed to know more about my Abba: why He loved me the way He did, what His promises were to me, what He required of me, what pleased Him and displeased Him. I needed to know His divine character. I figured that if I truly intended to live this Christian life, I was going to need all the information I could get on God in order to live it victoriously.

> YES, THE WORD BECAME MY PRECIOUS GEM, PRICELESS JEWEL, MY RARE GOLDEN COIN AND I KEPT THEM HIDDEN IN MY HEART.

My spiritual excavation started in the word of God—that is, the bible. Yes, *the* bible and, yes, you actually have to read it! As I dug, I found treasures upon treasures in the word of God. My study bible became my personal treasure chest. Along with consistent prayer for wisdom, knowledge, and understanding, it opened up a whole new world for me.

Suddenly, I was becoming spiritually rich; I began to see endless possibilities through the word of God. I was engulfed in the stories of the Good Book—the characters leapt off the pages. I was fascinated, envisioning each scene—feeling the heat from the burning fiery furnace in the story of Shadrach, Meshach, and Abed-nego. The pages became alive with fresh possibilities, love, hope, peace, joy, and faith. Yes, the Word became my precious gem, priceless jewel, my rare golden coin and I kept them hidden in my heart.

INTIMACY THROUGH THE WORD

Okay, so I know many of you may not be jumping for joy at the thought of reading the bible. But, there is no greater way to develop an intimate relationship with God and to know His character than through His words. Sure, go to religious seminars and conferences, go to church, buy the sermon CDs and DVDs and watch television ministries. But, at the end of the day, you must find out for yourself why it is called the Good Book and what is actually written in it. All knowledge of God, of who He is, is in the bible. The understanding of, belief in and adherence to His word is what draws us into an intimate relationship with Him.

> ALL KNOWLEDGE OF GOD, OF WHO HE IS, IS IN THE BIBLE.

While I am aware that reading the bible can be a daunting task, and it can be somewhat confusing, there is good news. We have, as born-again believers, the indwelling of the Holy Spirit. This acknowledgment, as a child of God, of the Holy Spirit is a huge part of living victoriously. It is the Spirit of truth, the Spirit of God that lives in us. Jesus promised believers that He would never leave us, that the Spirit of God would be with us at all times: "He will give you another Helper, that He may abide with you forever—the Spirit of truth, whom the world cannot receive, because it neither sees Him nor knows Him; but you know Him, for He dwells with you and will be in you. I will not leave you orphans" (John 14:16-18).

The Holy Spirit is multifaceted. It guides us in all things true and convicts us when we are not living according to the will of God. It is a discerning Spirit, a Spirit of wisdom, knowledge, understanding, revelations, and so much more. In fact, one of the functions of the Holy Spirit is to impart spiritual wisdom through scriptures: The "Spirit searches out everything and shows us God's deep secrets" (1 Corinthians 2:10), and as you read the bible, God will give you clarity and revelations through the Holy Spirit. I thank God for the Holy Spirit who is filled with an abundance of spiritual wisdom always available to us. But, I've also found a study bible to be helpful in my quest for intimacy with God.

A study bible is a bible that provides footnotes, word study, maps, historical facts, and a lot more. It breaks down some of the most complex scriptures into comprehensible nuggets of wisdom.

The study bible helped me *study* the word of God, as opposed to simply reading it. It has made a tremendous difference in the way I view the Word. It has now become my daily bread, through which I am able to see the visible manifestations of victory in my life.

When investing in a study bible, I suggest purchasing one written in today's language, which makes it easier to comprehend. A few suggestions are: New King James Version (NKJV), New International Version (NIV), the Amplified (AMP), the Messenger (MSG), and The New Living Translation (NLT). There are many great study bibles available in today's market. Do your research and choose the one that best fits your need.

READING VERSUS MEDITATING

It is important that you understand the distinction between "reading" the bible and "meditating" on the Word. Reading the bible is just that—reading the words. But, that does not mean that you've actually retained information or gained any insight into what you've read. Reading does not mean that the Word has taken root and if there are no roots, there can be no manifestations. On the other hand, when we *meditate* on the Word of God, we are essentially planting Word seeds into the soil of our hearts, which eventually take root. In time, those roots will spring forth a life visibly evident of the effectiveness of the Word.

> MEDITATING ON THE WORD NOT ONLY HELPS US DEVELOP INTIMACY WITH GOD, BUT IT ALSO SERVES AS A CATALYST FOR CHANGE—CHANGE OF HEART, CHANGE OF MIND, AND CHANGE OF LIFE.

The Hebrew word for meditate is "hagah," which means to mutter or murmur. It is the act of chewing over, mulling over, pondering, contemplating, considering, revolving, thinking over, and believing the word of God. When we move from merely reading the Word to meditating on the Word, it takes residence in our hearts, our spirit responds, the Word becomes a part of our subconscious minds, then a part of our conscious minds, and then it becomes life.

"Study this Book of Instruction continually. Meditate on it day and night so you will be sure to obey everything written in it. Only then will you prosper and succeed in all you do" (Joshua 1:8 NLT). Meditating on the Word not only helps us develop intimacy with God, but it also serves as a catalyst for change—change of heart, change of mind, and change of life. (See Pocket 3: Mind Games.)

As I meditated on the Word, Abba's character took form. Jesus, my friend, Lord and Savior's character took form. The Holy Spirit's character took form. I was being introduced and re-introduced to God every time I opened the bible and at every turn of the page. Grace, mercy, love, and faith were recurring themes, and the more I meditated, the more present they were in my life. There was no need for "self-help" books. No, I found everything I needed for life in the Word of God. The way I looked at it was: If Moses could part the Red Sea with the anointing of God, then how much more could He do for me in my life? Which seas did I need Him to part? Which paths did I need Him to make straight and clear? Meditating on the Word strengthened my spirit and brought me closer to God than I could have ever imagined.

INTIMACY THROUGH TIME

Developing an intimate relationship with God also requires spending time with Him in prayer. It is through prayer, through spending one-on-one time with God, that we commune with Him and are drawn closer to Him. (See Pocket 8: Arsenal of Victories.)

For many years, you may have sought God only when you were in need, but, now you are His child and He desires to hear from you. He desires to be involved in every facet of your life. He wants you to lean on Him, rely on Him, seek Him with all your heart. Your heavenly Father is the ultimate father and His love comes without measure.

> MAKE IT A DAILY HABIT TO SPEND TIME IN PRAYER, SPEAKING WITH GOD, SEEKING GUIDANCE FROM HIM FOR EVERY AREA OF YOUR LIFE.

In your time of need, in your time of despair, in your darkest times, He is there with open arms, and His "peace which surpasses all understanding, will guard your hearts and minds through Christ Jesus" (Philippians 4:7).

I've heard people say, "Do not question God." But I've discovered that there is nothing too big, too complex, too much for my Father to handle. God is able to handle whatever you are feeling—whether it is the pain from an abusive past, anger over the loss of a loved one, confusion about a situation. Whatever the emotions, do not be afraid to take them to your heavenly Father in prayer. God knows our thoughts before they are even formulated in our minds. He knows what we feel before we even have the opportunity to articulate our feelings. God is to be revered and feared (respected and admired), but I encourage you to be transparent with Him. Question in faith, respectfully express yourself, and in the process you may discover not only that He has all the answers you need, but that you have developed a deep bond, a deep fellowship with your heavenly Father.

Make it a daily habit to spend time in prayer, speaking with God, seeking guidance from Him for every area of your life, and soon you'll find that "in His presence there is fullness of joy" (Act 2:28). As mere human beings, we are naturally limited. But, with our Father's guidance, the possibilities for victory are unlimited.

LIFE AS A CHILD

So, child of God, know that from this moment on you will never be alone. From this moment on, God will be with you on this journey, sometimes carrying you, oftentimes leading you. You are royalty by virtue of your relationship to God. Hold your head up, stand tall, be bold, be confident, and know that even if your earthly father is absent from your life, your existence is not a mistake. You are fearfully and wonderfully made, and your heavenly Father loves you unconditionally.

Knowing who you are and whose you are is one of the major doors into a life of continual victories. I encourage you to start developing an intimate relationship with your Father. Get to know Him through His Word. Walk with Him and talk with Him daily. Lay all burdens on Him and He will carry them. Cultivate a real relationship with God, one that is not based on whether or not you went to church last week, or whether or not you've been good today, or whether or not you feel good today, or whether or not you got what you prayed for today. Cultivate a true relationship based on who you are: His child.

> FROM THIS MOMENT ON, GOD WILL BE WITH YOU ON THIS JOURNEY, SOMETIMES CARRYING YOU, OFTENTIMES LEADING YOU.

MAKE YOUR OWN NOTES

How do you view your relationship with God?

> "WE ARE HIS CHILDREN, GOD HAS SENT THE SPIRIT OF HIS SON INTO OUR HEARTS, PROMPTING US TO CALL OUT, "ABBA, FATHER.""
>
> ~ GALATIANS 4:6 NLT

POCKET
2

YOU WIN!

TANEKI DACRES

I've never considered myself a vindictive person or one to hold grudges. Sure, I have had relationships that have been severed due to betrayal, miscommunication, or some other reason. But, even then, in my heart I would always want the best for that person, and I would always forgive him or her. Always...well, except for my biological father and that one "special" someone. I just could not bring myself to offer those two individuals my precious forgiveness.

I grew up in a wonderful family of strong women, which included my mom, grandmother, aunts, and cousins. But unfortunately, like so many others, my father was an absentee dad. I was a shy fourteen-year-old girl when I finally met my father, and our relationship turned out to be nothing like my fourteen-year-old brain could have ever imagined.

> I WAS MORE THAN ANGRY; I WAS M.A.D.— MISSING A DAD.

I imagined being "Daddy's girl." I imagined looking into the eyes of the man who was so much a part of my being and seeing love. I imagined being able to call upon him for fatherly advice, to talk to him, walk with him, and feel his fatherly love. I imagined all this and so much more, but in reality, what I got was a man who initially seemed like he wanted to be a part of my life, but eventually began treating me like a stranger and a burden.

The years that followed our initial meeting were riddled with hurts, disappointment, headaches, and heartbreaks. I was no one's "Daddy's girl" and I was angry. Every chance I got, I cursed my father. I grabbed every opportunity to speak ill of him, to let the world know that he was a "deadbeat dad!" I was angry, and that anger turned to resentment, and that resentment turned to hatred. I was more than angry; I was M.A.D.—missing a dad.

This feeling of resentment was not made easier when, as I got older, the one man I truly loved did not reciprocate that love—or at least that's how I saw it. And now I had another person to feel resentful of.

He was everything I loved in a man—good looking, well-dressed, intelligent, ambitious and self-motivated. He was my "prince," but I was...just his friend. Now, if you have ever experienced anything like this, you know how painful this situation can be. Needless to say, my heart was broken and I felt the familiar hurt, pain, anger, and resentment all over again.

"I'm your daughter! You should naturally love me!" became "I'm the one who truly loves you! I've been there for you, so you should have loved me back!" My life was turned upside down, and inside out, and I could find no strength within me to forgive. I was shackled to the pain and resentment with no hope of release.

Since, thank God, I still had breath in me, life, though shackled, gradually resumed. After I experienced the anemia, pulmonary embolism, emergency surgery, pelvic hematoma, and dislodged IVC filter, I knew I needed to transform my life. I needed a rebirth. As I embarked on my spiritual cleanse, eventually I got to the most difficult part of the process: coming face to face with the spirit of forgiveness, or the lack thereof.

Coming face to face with unforgivingness was not something I was looking forward to. After all, I had gotten used to the shackles. They weren't tight anymore; I barely felt them and at times even forgot they were even there. My shackles were a part of who I was. They were my history and a part of my identity—that is, until I discovered my new identity in Christ.

While seeking God through His Word, I came across Matthew 6:14-15 (NLT), which says: "If you forgive those who sin against you, your heavenly Father will forgive you. But if you refuse to forgive others, your Father will not forgive your sins." As I continued seeking, I came across Luke 6:37 (NLT), which says: "Forgive others, and you will be forgiven." And, it was with that, ladies and gentlemen, that I experienced my first Holy conviction.

> I REALIZED THAT THIS BATTLE WAS REALLY NOT ABOUT HIM, BUT ABOUT ME BEING VICTORIOUS.

These scriptures sent conviction straight to my heart, and not only that, but the thought of not being forgiven by my Father because I had not forgiven others made me very, very nervous. Hey, I knew I was in no way, shape, or form perfect and I knew at some point—maybe even that same day—I would need God's forgiveness. So, I had a choice to make: obey the Word OR hold on to my old, familiar, rusty shackles.

Since I was undergoing a spiritual cleanse and taking on

a new journey, I chose the unfamiliar—I chose obedience to the Word. It was now time to face the past, but I was ready for this battle. Armed with the grace of God and the determination to be victorious, I tilted my hat, girded my waist, and stared all the wounds of my past straight in the eye, boldly declaring that at the end of this battle, I would win!

The battle began with a confrontation with the resentment I felt toward my biological father. I must admit that this was not an easy fight. There were many times during the struggle when I simply had to ask God to show me how to forgive my father. I wanted to please God, I wanted to obey His Word, but I simply did not know how to. "*He* was the one who chose to be absent from my life!" I'd say. "*He* was the one who hurt *me*! *He* was the one who should have assumed his fatherly duties! *He* should have been there for me! *He, he, he.*" And then I had an unforgettable "wow moment." I realized that this battle was really not about *him*, but about *me* being victorious. I was not forgiving him for his peace; I was forgiving him for *my* peace. With that revelation, my shackles began to break open and I had my first taste of freedom and victory.

With the taste of victory still so fresh, I quickly reengaged in battle and began confronting other areas of my life where there was pain, resentment, and strife. Forgive my "prince": Check! Forgive past friends: Check! Forgive all whom I perceived to have done me wrong: Check! Forgive, forgive, and forgive some more: Check!

I was a woman on a mission, and I was determined to

win. I began to search my heart and my thoughts for any areas that needed to be dealt with, anything that lay dormant. As each confrontation took place, I accepted each situation as is. I acknowledged that the circumstances were irreversible, forgave, and simply let go. Suddenly, I found myself completely free from the old rusty shackles that had kept me in bondage to my past. Suddenly I tasted sweet victory, and believe me, victory has never tasted so good!

> VICTORIES ARE WON NOT ONLY THROUGH CONQUERING OUR EXTERNAL BATTLES, BUT THROUGH CONQUERING OUR INTERNAL BATTLES.

After conquering my unforgiving spirit, naturally the next thing to do was to humble myself before God and ask Him to forgive my own sins. I wanted to "honor my father" (Ephesians 6:2 NLT), as the bible instructs. So, I sought God's forgiveness and repented for all the years that I cursed my father, all the years I spoke ill of him. I sought forgiveness and repented for every wrongful thought and ill feelings I may have harbored toward my "prince." I searched my heart and mind for every wrongful deed, word, or thought, sought God's forgiveness, and repented.

Again, I was a woman on a mission, determined to be victorious. What I've learned in combat is that victories are won not only through conquering our external battles, but through conquering our internal battles. In humbling myself, seeking forgiveness, and repenting, I discovered that I truly won the battle—I truly had the surpassing victory.

Simply Forgive

So here you are. You've given your life over to Christ; you now know for sure that you are a child of God, "an heir of God through Christ" (Galatians 4:7). You're trying desperately to embrace your newfound identity, but something seems to be holding you back. You haven't had an easy life. No, you have experienced some major struggles. You've been used, abused, neglected, abandoned, betrayed, lied to, cheated on, stolen from, mistreated, left for dead, and so on. No, your life has not been easy. You have been through it all, and you've seen it all, but now you're looking for a change. You see a glimmer of hope in Christ, and you know that if you look deeper and push harder, you'll eventually see a cornucopia of hope. But, there is something holding you back.

> YOU DESPERATELY WANT TO BREAK LOOSE, BUT THE GUILT, RESENTMENT, DISTRUST, AND PAIN KEEPS YOU SHACKLED. YOU SEE A NEW LIFE BEYOND THE HORIZON, BUT YOU JUST DON'T KNOW HOW TO GET THERE.

Each time you try to break free, you're pulled back by the memories of your past. You desperately want to break loose, but the guilt, resentment, distrust and pain keeps you shackled. You see a new life beyond the horizon, but you just don't know how to get there. You're in bondage. You want to experience life in a new way, and guess what? You can—it is not too late. If you relate to any or all of this, then here's some good news: There is a key available today, at no cost to you, which will set you free forever. That key is forgiveness.

Forgiveness is the master key that unlocks all the padlocks to the shackles of our past. It releases us from all the bondage of the past—all the heartaches, headaches, and pains. It sets us free and releases us to live victoriously.

Simply forgive. Forgive yourself and then forgive others. Your past is your testimony, but your future, whatever you make of it, is your destiny. Know that "what was intended to kill you, harm you, destroy you—God intended it all for good" (Genesis 50:20). Forgive and, in doing so, you will have chosen to live the life of a victor and not a victim.

Now, you may be saying, "But you just don't understand! I've been through a lot in my life, and I didn't deserve any of it!" And I am sure that you're right—you didn't deserve all that you went through. But, know that none of it comes as surprise to God. I know, had it been up to you, you would have chosen a different life for yourself, a different path. But God has brought you through it all, to this position in your life. Now, through your testimonies, others will be encouraged, inspired, and many lives will be saved (Genesis 50:20). Forgiveness gives God access to come into your life and use you in extraordinary ways to bless others.

Holding on to grudges, and harboring an unforgiving spirit is like having a wound that just will not heal. You've bandaged it over and over again, making sure to cover it up with your bubbly personality, with your charming smile, with your sense of humor. But, the minute you see that person, as soon as you hear the name of that individual, the second you smell the scent of that person, as soon as you have a flashback, the wound bleeds all over again with anger, resentment, pain, guilt, sadness and depression. It is now time to close that wound permanently. It is time to heal once and for all. It is time to forgive.

Forgiveness Is Not Weakness

There is oftentimes a misconception that forgiveness is a sign of weakness, and in an effort to not seem "weak," we allow the spirit of pride to take over our lives. We haughtily declare, "He'll have to rot before I forgive him!" or "I don't see why *I* have to be the bigger person!" or "I'm not budging. Let *her* make the first move!" But Proverbs 16:18 wisely informs us that "pride goes before destruction, and a haughty spirit before a fall...By pride comes nothing but strife" (Proverbs 13:10). Strife opens the door to bitterness, contention, struggles—shackles upon shackles.

> FORGIVENESS IS AN OUTWARD INDICATION OF TREMENDOUS INNER STRENGTH. IT TAKES A STRONG INDIVIDUAL TO STARE DIRECTLY INTO THE PAST AND DECLARE THAT "IT IS OVER!"

The "adversary, the devil" (1Peter 5:8) wants us to believe that to forgive is to be weak and by believing that, we are held captive by our past. But the devil is a liar. Not only should we have a desire to please God and be obedient to His Word, but we must recognize that forgiveness is an outward indication of tremendous inner strength. It takes a strong individual to stare directly into the past and declare that "it is over!" To declare that no longer will you be held in bondage. It takes a courageous person to rage against the past with the weapon of forgiveness. It takes a true warrior to choose not to be bounded by an unforgiving spirit. And that warrior is in you.

I cannot fully articulate how great it feels to experience freedom through forgiveness. There are no words that I'm able to find that truly describe how awesome it is to be able to think about my father and not feel anger, pain, or resentment. Words cannot explain how great it is to think of or even see my "prince" and not feel anger, bitterness, or sadness. The sense of freedom that one achieves through forgiveness is literally indescribable. It is restored power; it is restored control. No longer will one be able to have such crippling power over your life. No longer will you be shackled to your past. No longer will someone else be able to hold on to and play with your emotional strings. When you have chosen forgiveness, you have chosen to take back your power, to take back the controls, boldly declaring that YOU WIN!

> WHEN YOU HAVE CHOSEN FORGIVENESS, YOU HAVE CHOSEN TO TAKE BACK YOUR POWER, TO TAKE BACK THE CONTROLS, BOLDLY DECLARING THAT YOU WIN!

How to Start Forgiving

In order to start the process of forgiveness, you must first and foremost admit that there are areas in your life where you've yielded to an unforgiving spirit, areas where there are some unfinished business, so to speak. Initially, you may think, "I'm not harboring any grudges, strife or an unforgiving spirit," but there may be some things that have been lying dormant for years. Things that have shackled you for so long, that you have forgotten that they were even there.

> IF YOU DON'T SEE THE SHACKLES, YOU CAN NEVER BE FREE.

Start with prayer. Pray to God, asking Him to search your heart and bring to the surface any areas where there may be an unforgiving spirit, areas of grudges and strife that need to be dealt with. Think back to situations that may have caught you by surprise, situations that turned your life upside down. A friend may have betrayed you and, since then, you've seen every potential friend as a threat. An old flame may have hurt you and, since then, you haven't been able to trust or let anyone back into your heart. The situation could be anything that is holding you back, keeping you in bondage and away from an abundantly victorious life. Identifying these areas is a crucial part of the process, because if you don't see the shackles, you can never be free.

I had to think back to past friendship and relationships. I had to clear the mental clutter, clear the cobwebs of my mind, and simply get real with myself. I had decided that I was not going to let anything hold me back. I was going for the gold and nothing, including an unforgiving spirit, was going to sidetrack me. I was going to win!

The past is elapsed time, and we cannot change the circumstances of the past. Therefore, once you've identified the shackles that have held you back, come to grips with the reality of not being able to change what has already been done. No longer should there be any "woulda, coulda, shoulda." It is what it is—it is the past. Accept the circumstances as irrevocable and irreversible. Recognize that you have made it through and accept, truly accept that you do not have the power to change what happened. But, you *do* have the power to change how you live, how you view life, and to decide whether or not you will win.

Your past does not dictate your future, so be ready and willing to leave it behind. Isaiah 43:18-19 (AMP) reminds us: "Do not remember the former things, nor consider the things of old. Behold, I will do a new thing." Let it all go, forgive, and make room for God to do a new thing in you and your life.

Now, if you have identified the areas and accepted the past as the past, then great! You are on your way to truly living victoriously. But if you are finding this process of forgiveness difficult, if you just can't bring yourself to release, to let go, then I suggest you pray to the heavenly Father for His grace to help you change and forgive.

There are just some things that we cannot do on our own, areas that we find difficult to change, circumstances so huge that we find them difficult to face. But, there is nothing too big or too hard for God to handle. "His strength is made perfect in weakness" (2 Corinthians 12:9), and what we can't do with our power, He will strengthen us to do with His power.

Pray for the grace to forgive and the ability to let go of your past. God knows our hearts and sees our struggles. He sees a willing heart that may not know how to forgive. But as you continue to pray, and make efforts to change, His grace will guide you, and gradually you will be loosed. It may not be an overnight transformation, but soon there will be a metamorphosis and you'll have the freedom to fly above your circumstances.

"Love your enemies, bless those who curse you, do good to those who hate you, and pray for those who spitefully use you and persecute you" (Matthew 5:44). In addition to praying for the grace to forgive and let go, I also encourage you to pray for the souls of the ones who have caused you pain. "Wait, first you tell me to forgive, and now you are telling me to pray for the folks that caused all my grief?" you may be saying. "Oh, you must be crazy!" I can only imagine some of your responses. Believe me, it was no cakewalk for me either.

> THE WONDERFUL THING ABOUT THE GRACE OF GOD AND THE INDWELLING OF THE HOLY SPIRIT IS THAT BOTH WILL WORK TO CHANGE OUR CARNAL MINDS TO SPIRITUAL MINDS, MINDS THAT SEEK TO PLEASE GOD AND NOT OUR FLESH.

No, at first my prayers felt insincere. Although I had forgiven, I had not gotten to the place where I genuinely wanted to pray for them. I forgave them, but praying for them just seemed a little bit "too nice" for me. So, I quickly mumbled their names under my breath and kept it moving. But the wonderful thing about the grace of God and the indwelling of the Holy Spirit is that both will work to change our carnal minds to spiritual minds, minds that seek to please God and not our flesh (See Pocket 5: Sweet And Sour). As I continued to pray, the grace of God began to release my bindings. Eventually my prayers were not only sincere, but based on genuine love and forgiveness.

> THE UNFORGIVING SPIRIT HAS THE POWER TO CONTROL OUR EMOTIONS, ROB US OF OUR PEACE, AND VICTIMIZE US OVER AND OVER AGAIN.

Forgive and Be Free

One of the funniest and saddest things about holding grudges and malice is that oftentimes, while we are living miserably, the person to whom this energy is directed is totally oblivious to how we are feeling. He or she is living and loving life, while we are left holding on to the old rusty shackles. It is time to break free.

"When you are praying, first forgive anyone you are holding a grudge against, so that your Father in heaven will forgive your sins, too" (Mark 11: 25-26 NLT). Forgive and receive God's free gift of forgiveness through His son, Jesus Christ. An unforgiving spirit is not only disobedient to the Word and displeasing to God, but it also provides a doorway for the adversary to come in. Through this entry the enemy fuels us with anger, uncontrolled outbursts of repressed feelings, self-destructive thoughts, hatred, and a host of other emotions that, if left unchecked, may manifest into sickness and even death. The unforgiving spirit has the power to control our emotions, rob us of our peace, and victimize us over and over again. Believe me, nothing pleases the devil more than that!

It was through the act of forgiveness that Mary, a friend of my family, was able to experience true liberty and freedom after a turbulent, abusive past. Her past was filled with so much violence, tragedy, and chaos that, had it been a movie, it would have been a blockbuster.

Her past included being verbally and physically abused by her parents, being kicked out of her own home at a very young age, and being abused by a man whom she thought was her biological father only to find out at age fourteen, in a meeting with the school principal, that he was not a blood relative. Her past included witnessing the pain of her grandmother (the only person who showed love to her and her siblings), being kicked out of the home to "save her mother's marriage." It included being forced to eat spoiled, roach-infested food and risking violent beatings by sneaking off to her grandmother's home in order to have something decent to eat. Her past included being powerless to protect her younger sister, and having to stand by and watch her taken out of school and kicked out of the home because of an unexpected pregnancy. Her past included being gang-raped in her twenties, teetering on the brink of insanity, and suffering through the murder of her husband and childhood sweetheart two years into their marriage. Her past was meant to "steal, kill and destroy" (John 10:10) her life...but God!

It is only through the grace of God that this woman is still breathing. And the only reason she has her sanity is because she chose to forgive. Despite all that she has gone through, she forgave, and as result she is impacting lives through her testimony. Today she is free from all the shackles of her past, free to be the "salt of the earth" and the "light of the world" (Matthew 5:13-14).

The act of forgiving, whether oneself or another, is not an easy task, but it is necessary to experience true joy, peace, love, and victories. Choose to forgive, and gradually everything that has held you stagnant will break off from you. One by one, you'll begin to shed the events of the past, revealing a fresh, new, shiny layer of life.

There is power, freedom, peace and countless victories in forgiveness. Break free, break the shackles, and break the cycle. Claim your victory. In Jesus's name, YOU WIN!

MAKE YOUR OWN NOTES

Have you released yourself from an unforgiving spirit?

> "FORGIVE OTHERS, AND YOU WILL BE FORGIVEN."
>
> ~ LUKE 6:37 NLT

POCKET 3

MIND GAMES

"You are so sensitive!" I've heard this most of my life. Many people were warned, "Be careful what you say around Taneki; she might just get offended." Easily offended, emotional, always with a quick retort—that was me. I didn't back away and surely did not hesitate to give a piece of my mind. But, what could I say? I was a creative, emotional being! I'd been this way all my life and I didn't know how to change or even if I could change. This was who I was; this was my personality and how God made me. At least so I thought, until my rebirth.

> THE WORD BECAME THE BLUEPRINT BY WHICH I CONSTRUCTED THE TEMPLE OF GOD WITHIN ME.

When I became a born-again believer, everything in me said, "You need to change." I didn't want to be the same "sensitive" Taneki. I didn't want to think the way I thought, act the way I acted, or talk the way I talked. I wanted a fresh start, and the only way to do that was to get into the Word of God.

As I spent time in the Word of God, I began looking at the characteristics of a child of God—how to speak, act, and think. I began to transform with the Word, slowly changing who I thought I was to who He said I was. My knowledge about God increased, but so did my knowledge about the adversary, the devil.

I believed the Word and it transformed my life. I began to see life through a completely different lens. No longer was I affected by things, people, and circumstances the way I was before. The Word became the blueprint by which I constructed the temple of God within me. Each time I opened it, I found myself being refreshed, refined, and renewed.

Now, you are a born-again believer. You've received Christ as your Lord and Savior, but life is the same. You have the title of "Christian;" you've joined a few committees and ministries; Pastor So-and-So knows your name; you've bought a few books; you volunteer at the annual church praise-a-thon; you've attended a few seminars, but life, as you've known it, is still the same. When faced with the trials and tribulations of life, your reaction is the same as it was before—you're angry, depressed and hurt. You are still simply, an emotional wreck. You look the same. You have the same issues and habits. You talk the same. You have not changed, and neither have your circumstances. Well, this is it—there is one thing you've forgotten to do, and that is to renew your mind. Now, I'm sure you've probably heard it said before, but I'll say it again: It is time to renew your mind!

After you have identified yourself as a child of God, renewing your mind is one of the most important steps to take in order to live a life of victory through Christ. To renew your mind means to change your thoughts; it is the process of replacing wrong thoughts with the right ones. It is the act of aligning your thoughts with the Word of God.

Renewing Your Mind Is Critical

"Do not be conformed to this world; this age (fashioned after and adapted to its external, superficial customs), but be transformed; changed by the entire renewal of your mind (by its new ideals and its new attitude) so that you may prove, for yourselves, what is the good and acceptable and perfect will of God, even the thing which is good and acceptable and perfect in His sight for you" (Romans 12:2 AMP).

There is a war raging in our minds. The mind is the psychological function of the brain, able to produce memory, emotions, reasoning, thought, perception, imagination and communication. The average mind entertains fifty thousand to seventy thousand thoughts per day! We have thoughts upon thoughts, negative, positive, and indifferent—everything from "What should I eat for lunch?" to "I hate myself." In the course of five minutes we can go through a wide range of emotions, all due to our thoughts. In a very short period of time, we can think about an individual, have an imaginary conversation with him or her that turns into an argument, and decide that we will give him or her the silent treatment. All this can happen in our minds before we even have the chance to open our eyes, to see the morning sun; all without having to part our lips. No wonder the mind is the battleground of our lives! It controls what we do, how we do it, and how we feel about doing it. We think before we act, we think before we react, we think before we feel.

> WE THINK BEFORE WE ACT, WE THINK BEFORE WE REACT, WE THINK BEFORE WE FEEL.

Many of us believe that it is impossible to change our thoughts, and as a result we put up with feeling happy one minute and sad the next, angry one minute and depressed the next. We put up with basically being an emotional wreck. We believe that we "just can't help it" and resign ourselves to being "set in our ways," allowing our thoughts to take control and dictate the course of our lives.

Think about it. Have you ever noticed that when things go awry in your life; when you are disappointed, hurt, stressed or worried, your mind automatically throws a pity party? Suddenly you are bombarded with thoughts like "I can't see a way out of this" or "What am I going to do? I am doomed," or "What's wrong with me?" There is no rest, no peace of the mind, no sleep. If you manage to quiet your mind long enough to get some shut-eye and then awaken in the middle of the night, you are immediately flooded with anxiety and fear all over again. Is this something that only I have experienced? Or, have you ever gone to bed feeling happy, praising God, and expecting great things but felt a sense of doom, a heaviness in your spirit, the moment you woke up? If you've experienced anything similar to this, know that it is all a part of the war of the mind and the work of the enemy to agitate, disrupt and make you doubt the promises of God. The goal is to have you thinking outside of the will of God for your life.

> OUR THOUGHTS DICTATE WHO WE ARE, WHAT WE ARE, WHAT WE ARE ABLE TO DO, WHAT WE ARE CAPABLE OF HAVING, AND HOW FAR WE ARE ABLE TO GO IN LIFE.

"For as he thinks in his heart, so is he" (Proverbs 23:7). Our thoughts dictate who we are, what we are, what we are able to do, what we are capable of having, and how far we are able to go in life. Our minds are the enemy's playground and the battle that rages is between good and evil, light and darkness. The enemy's plan is to steal, kill, and destroy (John 10:10), and his strategy is to bombard our minds with negative, self-destructive thoughts. He is on the attack with a plan to steal our confidence, kill our dreams, and destroy our hope. He "walks about like a roaring lion, seeking whom he may devour" (1 Peter 5:8), guilefully waiting for every opportunity to infiltrate our minds with thoughts that are displeasing to God and outside of His will. His desire is for us to believe that we "will never make it," that we are "not strong enough," "not smart enough," and "not beautiful enough," that we are "damaged goods" and "not worthy," that God does not love us and is not here for us. But the devil is the father of all lies (John 8:44), and as children of God we have been given the weapon to defeat his wiles. We have been given the Word of God.

How to Renew Your Mind

So here you are, child of God. You're looking for a change. You want your life to be a reflection of a new life in Christ. You don't want to live the way you used to, speak the way you used to, or think the way you used to. Like Apostle Paul, "there is another power within you that is at war with your mind. This power makes you a slave to the sin that is still within you" (Romans 7:23 NLT). There is an ongoing battle in your mind and you don't know what to do. You want to have faith, but you think you're losing the fight. You've been knocked down so many times, and you just don't know if you have what it takes get back on your feet the next time around. Well, child of God, here is your solution—the Word of God.

Jesus said: "The words that I speak to you are SPIRIT, and they are life" (John 6:63), and Ephesians 4:23 instructs us to "be renewed in the SPIRIT of your mind, and...put on the new man which was created according to God, in true righteousness and holiness." The only way to truly experience lasting changes in our lives, the only way to win this battle that rages in our minds, is to renew our minds with the Word of God.

> EVERYTHING WE NEED FOR EVERY SITUATION WE MAY FACE IN LIFE IS IN THE WORD OF GOD. EVERYTHING WE NEED TO CHANGE WHO WE ARE, WHAT WE ARE, AND WHERE WE ARE GOING IS IN THE WORD OF GOD.

The Word of God is the will of God, and the basis for all victories through Christ. The Word is undefeated and the most powerful weapon given to believers to defeat the trickeries of the enemy. It is our weapon used "for pulling down strongholds, casting down arguments and every high thing that exalts itself against the knowledge of God, bringing every thought into captivity to the obedience of Christ" (2 Corinthians 10:4-5). The Word of God will never fail us. When we meditate on it, believe it, and allow it to take residence in our hearts, change becomes permanent and victory imminent.

Everything we need for every situation we may face in life is in the Word of God. Everything we need to change who we are, what we are, and where we are going is in the Word of God. Renewing our minds requires us to exchange our thoughts for God's thoughts, our beliefs for God's beliefs. It is knowing, believing, and accepting who God says we are, how He says we should live, and His promises to us.

The Word is "life"—it is the gateway to an abundant, victorious life through Christ. "The word of the Lord is tried" (Psalm 18:30 KJV); it is "pure" (Psalm 12:6); "the entirety of God's word is truth" (Psalm 119:160); it is a "great treasure" (Psalm 119:162); it is "good" (1 Timothy 4:6); it is health, healing, restoration—it is life!

> A THOUGHT CHECK LOOKS AT THE RELATIONSHIP BETWEEN THE THOUGHT AND THE EMOTION; IT CHECKS TO SEE HOW OUR THOUGHTS POSITIVELY OR NEGATIVELY AFFECT OUR EMOTIONS.

Renewing our minds is an ongoing process. It requires being conscious of our thoughts and doing what I like to call a "thought check." A thought check looks at the relationship between the thought and the emotion; it checks to see how our thoughts positively or negatively affect our emotions. Are your thoughts making you feel angry, sad, or anxious? Are you feeling joy and peace, or jealousy and hatred based on your thoughts? The goal of a thought check is to identify when our thoughts are not in alignment with the promises of God for our lives. By identifying when there is no peace associated with the thought, a thought check lets us know that the thought is outside the will of God.

It is not enough just to read the Word of God. We must also believe the Word of God. Every word must be believed and received within our spirits as truth. We have been given the authority, as children of God, to bring every thought into captivity—to reject worldly, self-defeating, wrongful thoughts and replace them with God's truth, which is His Word. Without the Word of God there can be no renewal of the mind. Without it there can be no change in our lives. Without it there can be no victories.

Here are four suggestions on how to start renewing your mind.

1) Know the Word of God. Meditate on the Word, believe it, have confidence in it, and have it "hidden in your heart" (Psalm 119:11). The Word is tried, tested, and proven. It is divine truth, life, and the only way to guarantee victory.

2) Conduct thought checks consistently in order to consciously be aware of wrongful thoughts and wrongful emotions. "God is not the author of confusion but of peace" (1 Corinthians 14:33). If there is no peace associated with the thought, it is not of God and therefore outside of His will. For example, thinking you are a "loser" will most likely trigger sadness and depression but not peace. Hence, the thought is outside His will for your life. Negative or wrongful emotions may be: anger, anxiety, sadness, depression, guilt, self-doubt,

jealousy, envy and a host of other emotions that rob us of God's divine peace.

3) Once you've identified negative thoughts, renounce them by declaring that they are not of God and rebuke the devil in Jesus's name. It is important to know that once you have submitted yourself to God, you have been given the authority to "resist the devil and he will flee" (James 4:7). We must not be afraid to renounce and rebuke the enemy. When Adam and Eve ate the forbidden fruit in the Garden of Eden, one of the first things God did was rebuke the work of the devil (Genesis 3:14). As children of God, we must follow suit—we must walk in our God-given authority, boldly declaring that we have the victory through the blood of Jesus. Remember the devil is the father of all lies, and his goal is to attack our minds with everything other than God's truth. What we must know, children of God, is that Christ has "crushed the head" (Genesis 3:15 NIV) of the enemy, giving him a blow from which he can never recover. The victory has already been won through the resurrection of the Anointed One. Resist, renounce, and rebuke the devil's attack to bring you down, destroy your life, and steal your hope. Walk in the confidence, boldness, and authority given to you by the blood of the Lamb and, like the enemy, these negative thoughts will flee.

4) Finally, replace the wrongful, negative thoughts by confessing aloud the Word of God and by confessing

positive, Godly affirmations. This is what I refer to as the "speaking life process." At this point the Word is being used like a "two-edged sword" (Hebrew 4:12), cutting and casting down every wrong, ungodly thought and destroying the plan and purpose of the enemy. To speak life is to confess the Word of God from your mouth and over your life. Whenever you are bombarded with thoughts like "I can't do this," "I'm just not qualified," or "I feel like a failure," you must resist, renounce, rebuke, and open your mouth to speak the Word of God as it relates to the situation. Declare with confidence, "No, this is not of God. Devil, you are a liar. I submit to God, I have the power to resist you and you will flee in Jesus's name. I rebuke you in Jesus's name. I'm a child of the most High God and I can do all things through Christ who strengthens me. I am more than a conqueror, and I have a surpassing victory in Christ Jesus. I know that all things work together for my good because I love the Lord and I am called according to His purpose!" According to Isaiah 55:11, "So shall My word be that goes forth from My mouth; it shall not return to Me void, but it shall accomplish what I please, and it shall prosper in the thing for which I sent it." God honors His Word; it shall not return to the Father void but will accomplish His will. Speaking the Word of God grabs the Father's attention, as well as the attention of the angels assigned to you. It is an indication to the Father that you are one who diligently seeks Him, believes Him, and knows Him intimately. Whenever the enemy says, "You can't do it," declare, "I am anointed to do all God has called me to do." Whenever he says, "You're not beautiful," declare, "No, devil, you are a liar. I am fearfully and wonderfully made. My Father did not make a mistake with me!" As you consistently resist, renounce, rebuke, and speak life, you'll experience a renewal of your mind, a change in your life, and changes in your circumstances. Know the Word, believe the Word, speak the Word, and renew your mind. (For more on Speaking Life, see Pocket 4: Watch Your Mouth!)

THE RENEWED MIND

Taking the time to renew my mind was the best thing I could have ever done on this journey. It was such a "wow moment" for me when I realized that I did not have to feel the way I did, I did not have to react the way I did, and I did not have to be as emotional as I was. The revelation that I did not have to allow my circumstances to "ruin my day" and cause me to "feel sad and depressed for the entire day" was mind-boggling and had me dazed with joy. Not only did I know who I was and whose I was, but I was walking in the power and authority given to me by virtue of that knowledge. Although I am forev-

> A RENEWED MIND IS A MIND FILLED WITH THE PROMISES OF GOD: A MIND OF HOPE, FAITH, PEACE, AND LOVE.

er a work in progress, life has no longer been the same since I discovered the awesome power of a renewed mind.

A renewed mind is a mind filled with the promises of God: a mind of hope, faith, peace, and love. A renewed mind is one that's strengthened by the Word of God, able to withstand the trials of life. It is one that sees every struggle as an opportunity for God to get the glory, for Him to reveal His awesome goodness. It is one that sees the glass half full as opposed to half empty. It is one that looks expectantly for supernatural breakthroughs, for the visible manifestations of the promises of God, and for the bounteous victories through Jesus Christ.

The renewal of the mind is not a one-time event but a lifelong process. As you continue to renew, it is important that you are mindful of the things that you are exposed to, the people you surround yourself with, and the places you choose to go. Why? Because it is simply counterproductive if, as you are praying to God for a breakthrough, every television program you watch only reports negative, dismal news and speaks constantly of an impending doom. It is counterproductive if you are working on renewing your mind and spirit through the Word, but the people you spend the most time with are always trying to convince you that "God does not care about you" or always trying to encourage you to live a lifestyle that you know in your heart is not pleasing to God. It is counterproductive if you are trying to believe and live by the Word of God but, you choose to go to the rock or hip-hop concert of your "favorite artist," whose every lyric is laced with profanity or speaks mostly of death, doom, violence, sex, or anything that may not be in alignment with where you see your life going.

It is imperative that, as children of God, we are mindful of what we are constantly exposed to, day in and day out. Because, whether or not you believe it, the fact is that whatever we constantly expose ourselves to, through sight or hearing, has a significant effect on our thought process and influences our lives, whether negatively or positively. Apostle Paul said it like this: "Set your mind on things above, not on things on the earth" (Colossians 3:2). Set and keep your mind on the promises of God. "Finally, brethren, whatever things are true, whatever things are noble, whatever things are just, whatever things are pure, whatever things are lovely, whatever things are of good report, if there is any virtue and if there is anything praiseworthy, meditate on these things" (Philippians 4:8).

> WE ALL HAVE A CHOICE: LIVE A DEFEATED LIFE OR LIVE AN EXPECTANTLY VICTORIOUS LIFE THROUGH CHRIST JESUS.

A continuous battle rages in our minds, but thank God that through Christ, we already have the victory. Every day we must engage with the Word and renew our minds. It is no longer okay for us to just have the title of "Christian." Our lives must truly be a reflection of one "belonging to Christ." We all have a choice: live a defeated life or live an expectantly victorious life through Christ Jesus. The choice is yours, but remember: "No one pours new wine into old wineskins" (Mark 2:22 NLT). We must renew our minds.

MAKE YOUR OWN NOTES

Has the Word of God changed your life and if so, how?

_____
_____
_____
_____
_____
_____
_____

> "DO NOT BE CONFORMED TO THIS WORLD, BUT BE TRANSFORMED BY THE RENEWING OF YOUR MIND, THAT YOU MAY PROVE WHAT IS THAT GOOD AND ACCEPTABLE AND PERFECT WILL OF GOD."
>
> ~ ROMANS 12:2

_____
_____
_____
_____
_____
_____
_____
_____
_____
_____
_____
_____

POCKET
4

WATCH YOUR MOUTH!

"Death and life are in the power of the tongue and they that love it, shall eat the fruit thereof" (Proverbs 18:21). I'm sure you've heard this scripture many times before, but take a moment to meditate on it until you truly grasp its meaning. *Death* and *life* are in the power of the tongue. The tongue, if you didn't know, is the movable organ in the floor of the mouth by which we eat, taste, and speak. Therefore, we have the power to speak death or life, and whichever we choose to speak regularly shall become manifestations in our lives; thus we "shall eat the fruit thereof."

> I REALIZED THAT MY OWN WORDS PARTIALLY PLAYED A ROLE IN WHERE I WAS IN MY LIFE, WHAT I HAD, AND WHAT I HAD GONE THROUGH.

The first time I heard a preacher repeat this scripture, I was not yet committed to God, but it had a tremendous impact on me. Being the analytical person that I am, I broke down every word and really thought about it long and hard. From that moment on I made an effort to take stock of what was coming from my mouth. I thought, "I don't want death to come from my mouth! I want life to flow from my lips!" I really tried for a while to speak life consistently, but my efforts lasted only so long, and soon enough I was back to the same old way of speaking. Now, I was never a negative person per se, but I wasn't reading the bible and hadn't renewed my mind. So, what the world said, I said. How the world spoke, I spoke. And that was just life.

It was not until I gave my life to God and read "but no

man can tame the tongue. It is an unruly evil, full of deadly poison. With it we bless our God and Father, and with it we curse men, who have been made in the similitude of God. Out of the same mouth proceed blessing and cursing. My brethren, these things ought not to be so" (James 3:8-10) that I thought, "Oh no, it ought not to be so at all!" It was then I began to think back—to analyze my speech patterns, so to speak. In doing so I remembered snippets of my past where I'd cursed my own life and the life of others with my mouth. I remembered moments when I expected the worst from situations and from others, moments when—for the sake of self-preservation—I consistently spoke negatively, even when my heart wanted a positive outcome. Moments when—out of the depths of hurt and an unforgiving spirit—I cursed my and others' circumstances. Suddenly I realized that my own words partially played a role in where I was in my life, what I had, and what I had gone through.

As I looked back, I saw visions of myself saying, "He's no good," "I know that's not going to work out," "He's not thinking about me," or "They are going to break up soon." It all played back to me like an old movie. And one day during my devotional, as I prayed to God regarding a particular relationship, God spoke into my heart and said, "How can you expect this relationship to work out when with your very lips, you've cursed another's relationship?" Now, let me just say, a revelation like that quickly knocks things into perspective. Eyes wide, jaw to the floor, I felt like I had just been slapped by the Holy Spirit. And with that, I humbled myself, asked for forgiveness, and repented.

Now some of you may think, "Well, *I'm* nothing like that!" Please don't misinterpret me: I was never one to live a life that involved constantly speaking negatively about myself or others. But, you know, when we gather with our friends and "say but not say," "gossip but not gossip"—"I'm just saying. I'm not gossiping. Just making an observation, that's all!"—it is at these times we unknowingly speak death into our lives and the lives of others. It is not something that we consciously do, but it is something that we do.

> SPEAKING LIFE IS THE MEANS BY WHICH WE MOVE MOUNTAINS, RESURRECT THE DEAD AREAS IN OUR LIFE, CHANGE CIRCUMSTANCES, AND EXPERIENCE LASTING VICTORIES.

Since my "holy slap," I've cleaned up my speech significantly, always trying to be mindful of what comes from my mouth. I am heedful of the words I speak about my life and the life of others. While some days are better than others, the Holy Spirit is always there to let me know when I am out of line, when I need to refrain, and when I simply need to shut up. (I love the Holy Spirit. He makes it so much easier to live the way God intends for us to live.) Today, I speak life.

LIFE VERSUS DEATH

To speak life is to speak according to the will and the Word of God. It is speaking words of blessings—words that build and uplift and that are beacons of light, hope, peace and love. It is the process by which we speak positive, Godly affirmations over our lives and the lives of others. It is the means by which we come into agreement with God and engage in self-prophesy, "calling those things which do not exist as though they did" (Romans 4:17). Speaking life is the means by which we move mountains, resurrect the dead areas in our life, change circumstances, and experience lasting victories.

> WE'VE SUBCONSCIOUSLY AND CONSISTENTLY SPOKEN SICKNESS, DEATH, HELL, AND DESTRUCTION INTO OUR LIVES.

On the other hand, to speak death is to speak contrary to the will and Word of God. To speak death is to come into agreement with the enemy—confirming with the fruit of our lips a life of defeat. It is the means by which we create strongholds and curses—yes, curses—into our lives and the lives of others. It oppresses, destroys, and is void of any specks of light, hope, peace, or love.

WHY LIFE?

"I have set before you life and death, blessing and cursing; therefore choose life" (Deuteronomy 30:19). Think about it: Speaking life should be something that comes naturally to everyone. After all, we all want the best for ourselves, our families, and our friends. We all want to be healthy, prosperous, strong, successful, grounded, loved, and all things good. But the sad and unfortunate thing is that we've become a society obsessed with death and destruction. Without a second thought, we have incorporated into our daily vocabulary words and phrases that are contrary to the will of God. We casually declare, "Hell yes!" to express agreement, "This is killing me" to express stress, "You make me sick" or "I'm sick and tired of this" to express disapproval, and "I laughed until I almost died" to express joy. And, the list goes on and on. So often we give the appearance of being believers and positive thinkers, quoting scriptures, making sure to attend bible studies, showing up to church bright and early every Sunday morning. But, when we are alone or among friends, we curse others and ourselves with the fruit of our lips.

We've subconsciously and consistently spoken sickness, death, hell, and destruction into our lives. When faced with trials and tribulations, we forget to "put on the whole armor of God" (Ephesians 6:13-17), to "fight the good fight of faith" (1 Timothy 6:12) and win. We've become children of God, sadly accepting life as is, surrendering in the middle of the enemy's attacks, living defeated, and not walking in our God-given authority. Through the fruit of our lips, we've weaved into the very fabric of our lives all things contrary to the will of God, and then we wonder why we haven't seen lasting victories.

Why speak life? Because "those things which proceed out of the mouth come from the heart, and they defile a man" (Matthew 15:18). Whether or not you agree, or whether or not you are aware, what we say is a reflection of who we are, and our lives are reflections of what we speak on a regular basis. Why speak life? Because "A fools mouth is his destruction."

Note: I'm *not* referring to anyone as a fool, but when we speak against the will of God, when we speak destruction, we reap destruction in our lives. Why speak life? Because the Word of God is "spirit" (John 6:63) and "God is a Spirit" (John 4:24), and when we speak the Word, we communicate spirit to Spirit. His promise is that His Word will "always produce fruit. It will accomplish all He wants it to, and it will prosper everywhere He sends it" (Isaiah 55:11). Why speak life? Because "whoever guards his mouth and tongue keeps his soul from troubles" (Proverbs 21:23). A loose tongue causes unexpected troubles in our lives. Why speak life? Because "the hypocrite with his mouth destroys his neighbor" (Proverbs 11:9). With the words of our mouths, we are able to cause unnecessary destruction in the lives of others. Why speak life? Well, I could go on and on, but let me end by saying: Speak life because speaking death should never be an option for the believer. In order to live victoriously, we must change the way we think, act, and speak. We must renew our minds and speak life!

> SPEAKING LIFE IS THE EVIDENCE OF A RENEWED MIND. BEFORE WE SPEAK, WE MUST FIRST THINK.

TIME FOR CHANGE

Children of God, it is time to change the way we speak. I understand that we are creatures of habit, but we should no longer speak the way the world speaks and act the way the world acts. We are in this world but we are not of this world

(John 17:16). If we do not change, we risk the chance of becoming "fruitless Christians," with nothing but a title to show for our walk with Christ.

Start changing the way you speak by acknowledging that you have been speaking against the will of God. Give it all to God, pray and confess. Now, it is *not* necessary to give God an itemized list of things you've said that may have displeased Him. Nor is it necessary to list every person's name you may have spoken badly about. But, it is good to confess that you've spoken outside of His will, and have committed sins that you are aware of and sins that you are not. "If we confess our sins, He is faithful and just to forgive us our sins and to cleanse us from all unrighteousness" (1 John 1:9). Once you've confessed, simply ask for forgiveness. Know by faith you've been forgiven, and repent. Remember, to repent means to have a change of heart, a change of mind. Now, the past is in the past, and it is time for a fresh start.

Speaking life requires us to know and believe the Word of God. Yes, everything goes back to the Good Book! It is not okay to simply speak positively. Any positivity without Christ as the foundation eventually crumbles, because it is not built on the solid "Rock" (1 Corinthians 10:4). Therefore we must know His promises for us, as they are the root of our faith.

Speaking life is the evidence of a renewed mind. Before we speak, we must first think, and this is why renewing our minds is so crucial. It requires us to have the Word hidden in our hearts, believing that the promises are made available to us. It requires us to claim those promises through the fruit of our lips.

POWER OF SPEAKING LIFE

It was through the mouth of God that the worlds were formed. God spoke humanity, the heavens, and the earth—all creation into existence. In Genesis 3-29, "*God said*, Let there be light: and there was light;" "*God said*, Let there be a firmament in the midst of the waters and let it divide the waters from the waters...and it was so;" "*God said*, Let the waters under the heaven be gathered together...and it was so;" "*God said*, Let the earth bring forth grass...and it was so;" "*God said...God said...God said...*and it was so." God spoke everything into being. The fruit of His lips is everything that we see around us. It's creation; it's life. His words are "living and powerful" (Hebrew 4:12). They are "spirit,"—which, by the way, is another word for "breath," which means "life." So God's words will always manifest life. When we speak the Word of God, we will always produce life in seemingly dead places, life in seemingly dead circumstances—physical, tangible, spiritual life—life in all forms.

> WITH THE FRUIT OF OUR LIPS WE CAN MOVE MOUNTAINS, AND NOTHING WILL BE IMPOSSIBLE FOR US.

When I think of the power of speaking life I'm often reminded of Ezekiel in the Valley of the Dry Bones (Ezekiel 37). If you can recall, God brought Ezekiel into a valley with dry bones and said to him, "Prophesy to these bones, and say to them, 'O dry bones, hear the word of the Lord! Thus says the

Lord God to these bones: 'Surely I will cause breath to enter into you, and you shall live. I will put sinews on you and bring flesh upon you, cover you with skin and put breath in you; and you shall live. Then you shall know that I am the Lord.'" Now, think about this for a moment. God is omnipotent. He could have simply breathed upon the bones, and they would have been restored. But instead He instructed Ezekiel to "prophesy," to "say to them." Why? Because there is power in speaking God's word. Essentially, He gave Ezekiel a firsthand look into what happens when we speak His powerful words over a seemingly dismal situation. It was a firsthand lesson on God's faithfulness to honor His word.

There is supernatural power in the Word of God, but we must start the process of speaking life.

SPEAK LIFE

Children of God, it is time for us to prophesy over the dry bones in our lives. It is time for us to speak life! With the fruit of our lips we can move mountains, and nothing will be impossible for us (Matthew 17:20). With the words of our mouths we can bind on earth and have it bound in heaven, loose on earth and have it loose in heaven (Matthew 18:18). We must believe the Word of God and faithfully appropriate it over our lives.

Start speaking life over your family. Declare, "As for me and my house, we will serve the Lord" (Joshua 24:15). Speak life over your children, even if they roll their eyes and have bad attitudes. Faithfully declare, "I have trained up my child in the way he should go, and he will not depart from it" (Proverbs 22:6). Declare that your children are the "upright and righteous," regardless of what you see. When the doctor diagnoses you with a life-threatening illness, faithfully declare, "By His stripes I am healed" (Isaiah 53:5) and continue to declare it. If you are unemployed, faithfully declare, "No good thing shall be withheld from me because I am the upright through faith in Christ Jesus" (Psalm 84:11). Speak life!

Faithfully declare, "I lack no beneficial thing because I seek—inquire of and require—the Lord" (Psalm 34:10 AMP); "My God will never leave me nor forsake me" (Deuteronomy 31:6); "My cup overflows with blessings" (Psalm 23:5 NLT); and "I'm anointed" (2 Corinthians 1:21). Declare with faith, "I am lacking nothing and needing nothing because my God faithfully supplies all my needs according to His riches in glory by Christ Jesus" (Philippians 4:19). When the spirit of fear grips you, declare, "God did not give me a spirit of fear but He gave me a spirit of love, power and a sound mind" (1 Timothy 1:7). In the midst of the storm, faithfully declare, "I have peace which surpasses all understanding because I've given it all to my Father" (Philippians 4:7) and "The Lord is my helper; I will not fear" (Hebrew 13:6). Declare, "I'm prosperous in all areas of my life" (3 John 1:2).

> WHAT HE SAYS IS OURS, IS OURS; WHO HE SAYS WE ARE, WE ARE; WHAT HE SAYS WE CAN HAVE, WE CAN HAVE. HIS WORD IS COMPLETE TRUTH.

Speak life into your finances, into your marriage, into your health, into your abilities, into your children, into your relationships. Speak life into every area of your life. We are His children, declared righteous through faith in Christ Jesus, and "the mouth of the righteous is a fountain of life" (Proverbs 10:11). When the world says, "There are no jobs; there is no hope," we should say, "I am favored and I lack no beneficial thing." When the world says, "It's crazy out there," we should say, "I have peace."

"We walk by faith and not by sight" (2 Corinthians 5:7), reminding God of His promises to us and believing by faith in Christ Jesus that what He says is ours, is ours; who He says we are, we are; what He says we can have, we can have. His Word is complete truth, but we will not experience supernatural victories in our lives until we begin to open our mouths with faith, and declare His promises—until we begin to speak life.

Whatever you may be going through, there is a scripture for you. Find the scriptures that relate to your circumstances, meditate on them, and declare them over your life *consistently*. Resist the habit or temptation to wrestle with your thoughts. You will never defeat the enemy if you do not open your mouth and engage the "sword of the Spirit, which is the word of God" (Ephesians 6:17). The word of God is "sharper than the sharpest two-edged sword" (Hebrew 4:12 NLT), and when we open our mouths and declare it with faith, barriers are torn down, pathways are made, and victory is won.

I've had some of the best conversations with myself—and

no, I am not crazy. But I've discovered that sometimes it's necessary to wait for those moments when we are alone to start declaring victories and breakthroughs into our lives. There have been many times when I have had to beat up the enemy, so to speak, by walking around my house declaring aloud, the promises of God over my life and my family's life. I do not have the time to wrestle with my thoughts. I have the sword, the Word. And whenever I am feeling anything *but* peace—anxiety, depression, doubt, worry—I quickly engage the "sword."

> A LIFE OF DEFEAT IS NOT FOR A CHILD OF GOD. BE CONFIDENT, BOLD, AND WALK IN YOUR AUTHORITY. SPEAK LIFE!

Your thought may be, "Well, I'm never alone." But, I suggest finding a closet to retreat in, or mumble the Word under your breath. There have been many times when I've been in a coffee shop, in a meeting, or just among the general public and I've had to mumble the Word of God under my breath and discreetly stifle the voice of the enemy.

Speak life while you're working, while you're cleaning, while you're driving, while you're walking, while you're washing the dishes, while you're mowing the lawn. Regardless of what you may be doing, just speak life.

"Out of the abundance of the heart the mouth speaks" (Luke 6:45). What's in your heart? What have you sown in your heart? Are you speaking in agreement with God or with the enemy? John 15:5 says, "Your own mouth condemns you, and not I; yes, your own lips testify against you." Has the fruit of your lips condemned your life? Start "sowing the word" (Mark 4:14) in your heart and declaring it from your lips. Speak life even if your "feelings" are not corresponding to the words that are coming from your mouth. Try not to be dissuaded by your "feelings," as they fluctuate—one minute here, the next there. Have confidence in the Word. God promises us that "He will not alter the word that has gone out of His lips" (Psalm 89:34). He said it and it is so. Have confidence and believe that God has "plans to prosper you and not to harm you, plans to give you hope and a future" (Jeremiah 29:11 NIV). Believe that "no eye has seen, no ear has heard, and no mind has imagined all He has prepared for you, simply because you love Him" (1 Corinthians 2:9 NLT). God is good and His word is always good. A life of defeat is not for a child of God. Be confident, bold, and walk in your authority. Speak life!

LIFE CONTINUES

Speaking life, like renewing your mind, is a lifelong process. It is "a process," meaning there is a continuation and some days you may be a force to be reckoned with, while other days you may fall a little short. That's fine, because "He who has begun a good work in you will complete it until the day of Jesus Christ" (Philippians 1:6). We are works in progress, and we will never completely tame our tongues. But that should never stop us from trying. This is a journey that, as believers, we must continue to embark on. We must make a conscious decision to speak life on a daily basis.

Choose to speak life and not death. Choose to speak blessings and not curses. Choose to speak words that build and not words of destruction. Choose to speak words that uplift and inspire. Choose to speak blessings and favor into your life and the lives of others.

> THERE IS NOTHING THE WORD CANNOT ACCOMPLISH WHEN WE SPEAK IT, BELIEVE IT, AND EXPECT THE VISIBLE MANIFESTATIONS OF IT.

There is nothing the Word cannot accomplish when we speak it, believe it, and expect the visible manifestations of it. God can do all things but fail, and His Word can do all things but fail. You have the power in your tongue to speak life and defeat the wiles of the enemy. You have the power in your tongue to speak victory into your life and the lives of others. Declare your victories in Jesus's name. Speak life!

MAKE YOUR OWN NOTES

Which are you speaking consistently: life or death?

> "I HAVE SET BEFORE YOU, LIFE AND DEATH, BLESSING AND CURSING; THEREFORE CHOOSE LIFE."
>
> ~ DEUTERONOMY 30:19

POCKET 5

SWEET AND SOUR

TANEKI DACRES

I am the type of person who does not like being told what to do. From very early in my life, I knew I wanted to be my own boss. There was just something in my DNA that screamed, "I want to do my own thing and not what you tell me to do!" I guess one could say I am a little stubborn. Sure, I listened to your advice but, would I have taken it? Not likely.

For many years I had no idea what the word "obedience" really meant. I remember on one of my darkest days—a day when I felt so low, so depressed—I had an encounter with one of God's servants. On that day, a stranger in a New York City train station prophetically said to me, "God will give you what you want, but you must be obedient." My thought was, "Obedient? How can I be obedient when I don't know how to hear from God, and have no idea what to be obedient to?!" It was several years later before I truly understood her prophesy and the meaning of obedience. And oh, what a blessing it has turned out to be.

> OUR OBEDIENCE WILL BE THE DIFFERENCE BETWEEN NO OR VERY FEW VICTORIES, AND A MYRIAD OF VICTORIES.

Obedience, I've discovered, is a natural part of life. The first people we are taught to be obedient to are our parents. And, if you grew up like some folks, you had to be obedient to every adult in your neighborhood. As we got older, we had to be obedient to teachers, bosses, clients, mentors, the law, and so much more. We say we are "free moral agents living in a free world, members of a society of liberated thinkers" but the reality is that everyone has someone or something to answer to. We may not want to view it as being "obedient," but we know that there are consequences if we do not comply. Yes, obedience is a natural part of life. And, as I've gotten older, I've come to realize that many of the people that I've had to answer to have been—dare I say it?—smarter than I am and have had my best interests at heart. I've also found this to be true within the Kingdom of God.

Now, I know, the word "obedience" is an ugly word. It is not widely used in our vocabulary, especially as we get older. But, it carries significant weight when it comes to living life victoriously through Christ. We are now children of God and, as such, there are things we do that please our Father and things we do that displease our Father. Our obedience will be the difference between no or very few victories, and a myriad of victories.

Obedience

Obedience is what I call the "behavioral aspect" of the spiritual journey. At this point we have begun renewing our minds and speaking life, but it's now time to put it all into action and behave like children of God. As much as we should strive not to speak outside of the will of God, we must also strive not to live outside of His will.

Obedience is the act of living life in accordance with the direction of the Holy Spirit, as well as with the Word, voice, and instructions of God. Obedience is the act of living according to the will of God and not our will. It is the means by which we walk in the Spirit and not the flesh.

Spirit versus Flesh

The Spirit and flesh are what I refer to as the Dr. Jekyll and Mr. Hyde personality of the born-again being. One is sweet, kind, loving, forgiving, peaceful, gentle, patient, honest, and good. The other, well, the other can be vengeful, spiteful, quick to anger, lustful, envious, selfish, deceitful, dishonest, and just not good. One says, "I love you," and the other says, "I hate her. She makes me sick." One—the Spirit—is our Godly nature, and the other—the flesh—is our "sinful nature" (Galatians 5:16). And much like the battle that rages in our minds, there is always a struggle between the two.

> WE ARE EMPOWERED TO WALK IN THE SPIRIT BY YIELDING TO THE SPIRIT OF GOD, ALLOWING HIM TO LEAD US, GUIDE US AND DIRECT OUR LIVES.

"The sinful nature wants to do evil, which is just the opposite of what the Spirit wants. And the Spirit gives us desires that are the opposite of what the sinful nature desires. These two forces are constantly fighting each other, so you are not free to carry out your good intentions" (Galatians 5:17 NLT). The flesh wants one thing and the spirit wants another. The flesh wants to hold on to grudges, offenses and unforgivingness. It wants to gossip, curse, be lustful, be envious, be deceitful—it is worldly. The Spirit, on the other hand, wants us to forgive and refrain from gossiping, cursing, and lustful behavior. It wants us not to be envious, not to worry; it wants us to surrender to the will of God—it is heaven-focused.

Now, at first glance this battle may seem like an impossible one to win. We may want to live for God, but that ole flesh just keeps getting in the way. Do not be dismayed. There is still hope for us yet, because Galatians 5:16 tell us that when we "walk in the Spirit, we shall not fulfill the lust of the flesh." So how do we walk in the Spirit? We walk in the Spirit by "letting the Holy Spirit guide our lives" (Galatians 5:16 NLT).

WALKING IN THE SPIRIT

When we were born into this world, we were born of the flesh—"conceived by our mothers and born sinners" (Psalm 51:5). But, when we were born again through faith in Christ Jesus, we were born "in the Spirit" (Romans 8:9). It is "the Spirit of God, who raised Jesus from the dead, that lives in us. And just as God raised Christ Jesus from the dead, He gives life to our mortal bodies by this same Spirit living within us" (Romans 8:11 NLT). As such, "we know that our old sinful selves were crucified with Christ so that sin might lose its power in our lives" (Romans 6:6). Therefore, through the Spirit of the living God, we are empowered to win the battle between the flesh and the Spirit. We are empowered to walk in the Spirit by yielding to the Spirit of God, allowing Him to lead us, guide us and direct our lives. When we yield to the Holy Spirit we yield to the will and Word of God; to the divine directions of the Holy Spirit. Walking in the Spirit is the way by which we live in this world, but not by the standards of this world.

When we walk in the Spirit we "put to death the deeds of the body" (Romans 8:13), choosing to be led by the Holy Spirit and not by our sinful natures. "To be spiritually minded is life and peace" (Romans 8:6). Like everything else in the Kingdom of God, we reap what we sow, and when we walk in the Spirit we bear the fruit of the righteousness of God in our lives. Our lives, our attitudes and behaviors, will reflect the Spirit of God that lives within us. The Holy Spirit will produce the fruit of "love, joy, peace, patience, kindness, goodness, faithfulness, gentleness, and self-control" (Galatians 5:22-23), and that's when we will begin to hear, "I don't know, but there is something different about you." That "something," dear friends, is the fruit of the Spirit—Christ reflected through us.

> WHEN WE WALK IN THE SPIRIT, GOD IS FAITHFUL TO OPEN DOORS THAT NO MAN CAN CLOSE.

There are many ways that the Holy Spirit will guide us, but mostly He'll guide us through the Word—communicating through revelations, directing us through scriptures. He will also guide us by speaking directly into our spirit. That's when we "feel something is wrong—I don't know what it is, but I feel it." That's when we feel an uneasy stirring, an inclination in our spirits to do something or not do something. He will also guide our decisions by speaking to us with a strong sense of divine peace. That's when we may be facing a difficult situation and suddenly the thought "Call Mike; he will be able to help" pops into our minds, along with a strong divine peace, assuring us that all will be well.

The Holy Spirit will always guide us, but we must yield and be obedient to His leadership. When we walk in the Spirit, God is faithful to open doors that no man can close, bless us with opportunities beyond anything we could have possibly imagined, and shower us with many victories.

Walking in the Flesh

Walking in the flesh, on the other hand, is being alive to sin—walking contrary to the Spirit, Word and the will of God. It is being dominated by our sinful nature, being controlled by our sinful desires. It is a carnal mind that is set on fleshy desires and sinful things. It is doing what we want to do, when we want to do it, with no regard. It is living a life of disobedience to the Spirit of God, living by the world's standard—living a life built on self-gratification, self-loathing, and selfish desires.

> WALKING IN THE FLESH CONSISTENTLY WILL ALWAYS TAKE OUR LIVES DOWN THE PATH OF DESTRUCTION.

Walking in the flesh is doing what we know in our hearts we should not do, or what we know is displeasing to God but choose to do it anyway due to lust, envy, hatred, jealousy, and a host of other sinful emotions. "When we follow the desires of our sinful nature, the results are very clear: sexual immorality, impurity, lustful pleasures, idolatry, sorcery, hostility, quarreling, jealousy, outbursts of anger, selfish ambition, dissension, division, envy, drunkenness, wild parties, and other sins like these" (Romans 5:19-21 NLT). "The sinful nature is always hostile to God. It never did obey God's laws, and it never will. Those who are still under the control of their sinful nature can never please God" (Romans 8:7-8 NLT).

"For to be carnally minded is death" (Romans 8:6). Walking in the flesh consistently will always take our lives down the path of destruction. At first, our fleshly desires may seem harmless. "Oh, live a little!" we might say. "Life is short and you only live once. You might as well live the way you want to!" But eventually, a life controlled by our sinful natures will lead us to binds, bondages, curses, shackles, and death—death of friendships, marriages, dreams, spiritual death, and everything else. Our lives will always be a direct reflection of the choices we make on a regular basis.

A Reflected Walk

There are consequences for everything we do in life. We may not like it, or want to even think about it, but it is a universal truth. When we misbehaved as a child, there were consequences. When we violate company policy, there are consequences. When the client asks us for one thing, and we present him or her with another, there are consequences. The same is true for the Kingdom of God. There are consequences for walking in the flesh and living a life of disobedience.

God knows that we are not perfect, and He knows that we will never be perfect. He knows that because Kerry walked by without greeting us, we may decide to give her the cold shoulder. He knows that Bob is getting on our "last nerve," and the next time he says something we just may lose it. He knows that we may roll down our car windows and tell that driver, who just cut us off, a thing or two. He knows that there is a constant battle between the Spirit and the flesh, and it is with this knowledge, along with His deep and abiding love for us, His children, that He has given us both His Word and His Spirit to empower us, so that we have "no obligation to do what our sinful nature urges us to do" (Romans 8:12 NLT). Therefore, "to whom much is given, from him much will be required; and to whom much has been committed, of him they will ask the more" (Luke 12:48). In other words, we know better; we do better.

> HABITUAL DISOBEDIENCE IS THE DOORWAY THROUGH WHICH THE ENEMY COMES IN AND WREAKS HAVOC ON OUR LIVES.

We have the Word and we have the Spirit, and as a result we must refrain from consistently drawing on the "grace card" to justify our disobedience. We must no longer claim, "Well, God knows my heart," for a habitual life in the flesh. Grace is wonderful—it is the favor and love of God we receive when we least deserve it or have done nothing to earn it. That's how much He loves us. It is a free gift from God, but it is not to be considered a free-for-all ticket to sin. "Do not be deceived, God is not mocked; for whatever a man sows, that he will also reap. For he who sows to his flesh will of the flesh reap corruption, but he who sows to the Spirit will of the Spirit reap everlasting life" (Galatians 6:7-8). The reality is that "we are slaves to whatever we choose to obey. We can choose to be a slave to sin which leads to death, or we can choose to obey God, which leads to righteous living" (Romans 6:16).

Habitual disobedience is the doorway through which the enemy comes in and wreaks havoc on our lives. When we consciously and consistently choose disobedience, we fall from grace and are subjected to consequences, such as curses, poverty, destruction, and delayed blessings. In fact, Deuteronomy 28 gives us an extensive list of the blessings of obedience and the curses of disobedience. The list for the curses of disobedience includes poverty, captivity, sickness, destruction, plagues, torment, failure, binds, bondages, yokes, defeat, humiliation, fear and so much more. The scripture wisely warns us by saying, "If you refuse to listen to the LORD your God and to obey the commands and decrees he has given you, all these curses will pursue and overtake you until you are destroyed" (Deuteronomy 28:45 NLT). Now, I don't know about you, but I like the good life, and this scripture has truly placed the fear of God in me. This is a scripture that should make us all want to pull up our bootstraps and walk in obedience. But this is not the only scripture that warns us about a disobedient life. Oh no, the Word has many more to offer us.

Throughout the bible are accounts of the repercussions of habitual disobedience—accounts of lives perishing, barrenness, captivity, discontinuation of resources, death of livestock, and more. "If you are willing and obedient, you shall eat the good of the land; but if you refuse and rebel, you shall be devoured by the sword" (Isaiah 1:19). Habitual disobedience cuts us off from the abundant resources of our Father; it causes floods of blessings to be dried up within an instance and cuts us off from the provisions of God. It breaks the covenantal relationship with our Father and leaves us vulnerable to the traps, trickeries, and deception of the enemy.

When we choose to walk in the flesh and be disobedient, we unknowingly create chaos and problems in our own lives. We have, from time to time, through disobedience, brought trials upon ourselves that we could have avoided had we been obedient to the Spirit within us. Think about it. Reflect for a moment on some of the decisions you may have made contrary to what you felt in your Spirit to be right. Have you ever taken a job that you knew in your Spirit was not the right job for you, telling yourself, "The economy is so bad and there's no hope"? Did you rationalize the decision only to have it end in disaster? Or, have you ever dated someone that you felt in your Spirit was not right for you but, because you didn't want to be alone or because you

> WE HAVE, FROM TIME TO TIME, THROUGH DISOBEDIENCE, BROUGHT TRIALS UPON OURSELVES THAT WE COULD HAVE AVOIDED HAD WE BEEN OBEDIENT TO THE SPIRIT WITHIN US.

were merely bored, you decided to go ahead—only for it to be the biggest headache and heartache of your life? Or, have you ever felt in your Spirit that you needed to apologize to someone, but because of the spirit of pride, you refused to submit to the urging of the Holy Spirit and, as a result, lost one of your dear friends? If you have, you are not alone.

We have all done things contrary to the move of the Holy Spirit. Before we were saved, we referred to it as "something told me…" Most of us have experienced that small still voice in the back of our minds saying, "No, don't do it. Run for the hills!" Yet, we did it anyway and reaped unfavorable results. It is times like these we lament, "Why did this happen to me?" or "If I had only known" or "Lord, why did You allow this?" But in reality, *we* were the ones who opened the door to disappointments, failures, and pain through our disobedience. It is only by the grace of God that we've survived some of the decisions we've made out of the flesh.

God knew that this walk would not be easy, and that's why He gave us His Word and His Spirit to guide us on this journey. He has given us a choice: Choose the Spirit and reap the wonderful things of the Spirit, or choose the flesh and reap all that comes along with it. The choice is ours to make.

BEING DOERS

It is imperative that we strive to "be doers of the word, and not hearers only, deceiving ourselves" (James 1:22). To know the Word of God and not apply the Word "is like glancing at your face in a mirror. You see yourself, walk away, and forget what you look like. But if you look carefully into the perfect law that sets you free, and if you do what it says and don't forget what you heard, then God will bless you for doing it" (James 1:23-25 NLT).

> BEING DOERS, BEING OBEDIENT TO THE WORD, AND ALLOWING OUR LIVES TO BE LED BY THE HOLY SPIRIT MAKES US PARTAKERS OF THE COVENANTAL RELATIONSHIP AND THE RECIPIENTS OF AN ABUNDANTLY BLESSED LIFE.

The Word of God and the Holy Spirit are not given for our entertainment—they guarantee us life and life more abundantly. The Word is the blueprint to the good life. It is the Kingdom's policy handbook, providing us with guidelines on how to speak, how to think, how to act, how to interact—how to live a life in Christ.

The Holy Spirit is the Kingdom's supervisor, keeping us in line, giving us directions, showing us where we may have gone wrong, and giving us the spiritual tools to live according to the Kingdom's policies. Being doers, being obedient to the Word, and allowing our lives to be led by the Holy Spirit makes us partakers of the covenantal relationship and the recipients of an abundantly blessed life.

LOVE, NOT LAW

When we think about obedience, we often think of the Ten Commandments, otherwise known as God's law. The thought of having to abide by all these laws may make us feel like we are walking on eggshells, it can be a little daunting. But, thanks to our Lord and Savior Jesus Christ, all these commandments can be summed up into one commandment, and that's the commandment to love: "You shall love the Lord your God with all your heart, with all your soul, with all your mind, and with all your strength. This is the first commandment. And the second, like it, is this: You shall love your neighbor as yourself. There is no other commandment greater than these" (Mark 12:30-31).

> FAITH SAVES US, BUT OUR BLESSINGS ARE THE FRUIT OF OBEDIENCE.

This is the commandment to love, upon which all the other commandments hang. For according to Romans 13:10 (NLT), "Love does no wrong to others, so love fulfills the requirements of God's law." Our adherence to the commandment to love is what pleases God most, and when we walk in love, we will not yield to our sinful natures. Yet, abiding by this single commandment is, at times, one of the hardest things to do—in particular the requirement to love our neighbor as ourselves.

Let's face it: Loving another can be challenging at times, especially if you and that "neighbor" have opposing personalities or cultural, religious, or generational differences. It is oftentimes difficult for us to let go of our preconceived notions of others. It is difficult at times to let go of grudges, to forgive and genuinely bless those who curse us. It is challenging but not impossible. When we push beyond our flesh, when we yield to the Spirit, submit and surrender to His will, the grace of God will empower us to walk in obedience to love. There is nothing that God will ever say to us, or require of us that He is not able to empower us, through His Spirit, to do.

1 Corinthians 13-1-3 (NLT) tells us, "If I could speak all the languages of earth and of angels, but didn't love others, I would only be a noisy gong or a clanging cymbal. If I had the gift of prophecy, and if I understood all of God's secret plans and possessed all knowledge, and if I had such faith that I could move mountains, but didn't love others, I would be nothing. If I gave everything I have to the poor and even sacrificed my body, I could boast about it; but if I didn't love others, I would have gained nothing." Without love for others, this journey would be worth nothing. Christ is love and we belong to Him, therefore our lives should be a reflection of His love for us.

The enemy's goal will always be to take us out of love and have us walking in the flesh. Every attack, every battle, is his attempt to sever love, and destroy or prevent relationships. His strategy is to play on our insecurities and plant seeds of offense: "I don't like her" you say, yet you've never had a conversation with her. "I didn't like the way he just looked at me" you say, and suddenly you are walking in disobedience to the commandment to love. The enemy's strategy is to steal, kill and destroy our love for God, ourselves, and others. Resist, renounce, rebuke, and choose love!

The Spirit Is Life

Faith saves us, but our blessings are the fruit of obedience. When we walk in the Spirit and live a life of obedience, Deuteronomy 28:1-14 tells us that "wherever we go and whatever we do, we will be blessed." It tells us that we will see our enemies defeated, that we will be elevated, that we will have prosperity and prosper in everything that we do, that our children will be blessed, and that there will be an abundance and overflow of provisions in our lives. It promises us that "the LORD will make us the head and not the tail, and we will always be on top and never at the bottom." These are the blessings of obedience; these are the promises of God to His children when we yield to the Holy Spirit and to His will

Obedience should never be considered a burden; it should be a desire to please the Father, for we know that "those who are in the flesh cannot please God" (Romans 8:8). God has been good and continues to be good to us, even when we are not good toward Him. He is faithful to us, and therefore our obedience should be born out of our sincere love and appreciation for Him. It should be born from knowing our identities, developing an intimate relationship with Him, and experiencing His immeasurable love for us and grace toward us.

When we were in the world and of it, we were blinded by the fruit of our sins. But now, through God's love and grace, we have been redeemed, set free, reconciled as His children and the "the veil has been taken away" (2 Corinthians 3:16).

As such, we must strive to live a life of obedience, one led by the Holy Spirit. Every day may not go according to plan, some days we may fall short of obedience, but with the grace of God, each morning presents us with another opportunity to get it right.

> YOUR OBEDIENCE WILL BECOME A REFLECTION OF CHRIST WITHIN YOU. YOUR LIFE WILL BEAR THE FRUIT OF THE RIGHTEOUSNESS OF GOD, AND YOU WILL BE OVERTAKEN BY THE BLESSINGS OF OBEDIENCE.

"There is no condemnation for those who are in Christ Jesus, who do not walk according to the flesh, but according to the Spirit" (Romans 8:1). Jesus loves you whether you walk in the flesh or the Spirit, but it is the Spirit that pleases Him. Pray daily for His grace to walk in the Spirit and not in the flesh. Think of obedience as an opportunity to express your love for God. As you continue this journey, your obedience will become a reflection of Christ within you. Your life will bear the fruit of the righteousness of God, and you will be overtaken by the blessings of obedience. Walk in the Spirit, and you will experience exceptional victorious through Jesus Christ. The choice is yours. Hint: Choose the Spirit!

MAKE YOUR OWN NOTES

What areas of disobedience you are struggling with?

_____
_____
_____
_____
_____
_____
_____
_____

> "TO BE SPIRITUALLY MINDED IS LIFE AND PEACE."
>
> ~ ROMANS 8:6

_____
_____
_____
_____
_____
_____
_____
_____
_____
_____
_____
_____

POCKET 6

THE GOOD FIGHT

TANEKI DACRES

As a child, my mother would always say to me, "The sky is the limit." And being the visual person I am, I visualized the sky and thought, "I don't see a limit to the sky." That translated in my mind that the possibilities were endless—I could do anything I put my mind to. Anything! If I wanted to be the president, I could, because my mother said, "The sky is the limit." If I wanted to be a pilot, I could, because my mother said, "The sky is the limit." Whatever I wanted to do, whatever I wanted to be, I believed I could, because my mother said, "The sky is the limit." I have carried these five simple words with me throughout my life.

> I BELIEVED IN GOD AND PRAYED TO HIM, BUT MY FAITH FLUCTUATED BASED ON MY CIRCUMSTANCES AND EMOTIONS RULED MY LIFE.

As I got older and began to find my place in this world, I would always remind myself, "The sky is the limit." This belief fueled my passion for entrepreneurship, and at twenty-three years of age I started my first venture, an online magazine. I had plans of being a multimillionaire by age thirty and retiring by age forty-five. Yes, I had big, big plans, and it was all going smoothly until my business partner and I stopped seeing eye-to-eye. Despite my "can do" attitude, the magazine went under after a year. The failure of the magazine was disappointing, but not devastating, because I still believed, "The sky is the limit." So, I dusted myself off and moved on. I moved on and I moved on, but nothing seemed to work out the way I had planned. Like that of so many others, my faith was tested throughout the years.

I believed in God and prayed to him, but my faith fluctuated based on my circumstances and emotions ruled my life. I was not yet a born-again believer. I had not renewed my mind, and so I was still a self-proclaimed "emotional being." I tried thinking positive thoughts and sought God in the middle of the storms. I may not have given my life to Him, but I sought Him and held on to what was now a whisper: "The sky is the limit." I tried believing for the right outcome, but when the right outcome morphed into the wrong outcome, my faith faltered. For many years that was the cycle: Happy and positive ("Yeah! This is going to be great!"), to sad and negative ("Nothing is going right"), and back again.

One of the most difficult periods of my life was when I purchased a well-known fast-food franchise restaurant. I was twenty-seven and had no experience in the fast-food industry, but I had a vision and a plan. I worked hard to see the restaurant open—created my business plan, secured loans, found the location, had the building constructed. I worked hard with a vision and plan in hand, and eventually my restaurant was open for business. This was one of my proudest moments. "I did it!" I thought. "My mom was right; the sky truly is the limit. And, the best is yet to come."

As I settled into the role of franchise owner, still thinking positive thoughts, I quickly discovered how overwhelming the day-to-day management of a restaurant can be. Soon I found myself struggling to keep the restaurant open and maintain a roof over my own head. I was drowning in debt—from employee payroll, rent, insurance, food, taxes, franchise fees, loan repayments, and so much more. "The sky is the limit" was again a mere whisper fading away and I began sinking into a deep depression.

I would spend days locked in my apartment, windows closed, curtains drawn, in complete darkness physically, spiritually, and mentally. The restaurant was supposed to be my stepping stone to greater things, but it became a quick-quicksand filled with stress. It was then that I really began to seek God. I needed something or someone to hold on to; I needed a lifeline.

> I BELIEVED EVERY WORD IN THE BIBLE —EVERYTHING IT SAID I WAS, WHAT IT SAID I COULD DO, WHAT IT SAID I COULD HAVE. EVERYTHING IN IT WAS FOR ME AND ABOUT ME, AND I BELIEVED IT.

I would lie at night crying, praying to God, and seeking His direction. I felt His peace surround me, as if I were being embraced in the arms of a loving Father comforting me, gently rocking me to sleep.

Eventually, one morning, after a night of praying and crying, I stepped out of my apartment and bumped into a fellow entrepreneur who had recently closed his business, which had been in the same neighborhood as mine. He explained to me that before going into business, he had been a banker and when he began to look at the numbers after several years of running his business, "they were not adding up." He then turned to me and said, "I don't know what's going on with you, but sometimes we need to give up certain things in order for God to bless us the way He really wants to bless us." I immediately knew, in my heart, that this was not a chance encounter but one divinely orchestrated by God.

I eventually sold the restaurant, but the experience left an indelible mark in my life. It was through this experience I saw firsthand the grace of God upon my life. Through this experience, my faith in God was strengthened—but it was not solidified, because I simply did not know the Word of God. I knew how to pray to God in time of need but I did not truly know Him. So as life continued, and I was faced with many different trials and tribulations—outstanding debt, betrayal, persecution, delays, failures, and sickness—my faith was tossed to and fro, up and down by the waves of life. My faith was not stable, because it was built on "positive thoughts" and "good energy." And while both are great, my faith was still missing the solid foundation—the Word of God.

> WHAT I DO KNOW FOR SURE IS THAT EVERYTHING I THOUGHT WAS A DELAY WAS GOD'S WAY OF TEACHING ME, AND PREPARING ME FOR THIS SEASON OF MY LIFE.

My faith grew exponentially during my spiritual journey. It was then that I began not only reading the Word, but also believing the word of God. The old, analytical Taneki went out the window. I was not trying to rationalize the Word—I simply read it, mediated on it, and believed it. I believed every word in the bible—everything it said I was, what it said I could do, what it said I could have. Everything in it was for me and about me, and I believed it.

When I read, "Ask, and you will receive, that your joy may be full" (John 16:24), I believed it. When I read, "By His stripes we are healed" (Isaiah 53:5), I believed it. When I read, "I can do all things through Christ who strengthens me" (Philippians 4:14), I believed it. The word became my daily bread—my sustenance, keeping me healthy and strong. Whatever the word said, I believed. And as I believed, I was strengthened from faith to faith.

Today I still believe that the sky is the limit, but my faith has been solidified by the Word of God. As I look back, I can clearly see how God had a hand in every area of my life. In the process, I learned so much about my Father, faith, trust, and God's desires. Was the franchise God's desire for my life? Maybe or maybe not—I will never know. At the time, I did not stop to ask what His desire was. What I do know for sure is that everything I thought was a delay was God's way of teaching me, and preparing me for this season of my life.

Jesus said in John 6:45, "Everyone who has heard and learned from the Father comes to Me." Every failed business venture, every setback, every failure, every distraction, every sickness drew me closer to Him. Every time I lay crying, trying to figure out how to pay my employees, how to pay the rent for my restaurant, how to keep the lights on, how to pay the vendor, how to keep a roof over my head—all of these moments prepared me for this stage in my life. And, the same may be true for your life.

You may be going through a difficult period. Maybe you've had some very rough years and your faith has been truly tested. You may be stuck in between worlds—you want to believe the Word, but the world keeps telling you, "Seeing is believing" and "Believe it when you see it." And the way things are going in your life, you are swaying toward the world's side. But, children of God, "God has chosen us out of this world" (John 15:19) and "blessed, happy and to be envied are those who have never seen Jesus and yet have believed, adhered to, trusted and relied on Him" (John 20:29 AMP). Faith and trust in God are the keys that unlock the door to remarkable blessings and victories. So, when the world says, "You have to see it before you believe it," boldly declare, "I am a child of God. I walk by faith and not by sight!" (2 Corinthians 5:7).

> FAITH AND TRUST IN GOD ARE THE KEYS THAT UNLOCK THE DOOR TO REMARKABLE BLESSINGS AND VICTORIES.

AUTHOR AND FINISHER OF FAITH

In talking about faith, we must first begin with the "author and finisher of our faith, Jesus Christ" (Hebrews 12:2). Our faith begins and ends with Jesus, as it is through His work on the cross that we are saved and the promises of God are made available to us, His children.

Without Jesus, our prayers would go unanswered. Without Jesus, we would not be able to enter the presence of God and make our requests be known to Him. In fact, prior to Jesus the only person allowed to enter the presence of God was the high priest. If any man other than the high priest had entered, he would have died. Hebrew 9:7 tells us that "only the high priest ever entered the Most Holy Place (the true presence of God), and only once a year. And he always offered blood for his own sins and for the sins the people had committed in ignorance."

> IT IS OUR FAITH IN JESUS THAT POSITIONS US TO RECEIVE THE SUPERNATURAL BLESSINGS. IT GIVES US THE CONFIDENCE TO EXPECT EVERYDAY MIRACLES IN OUR LIVES. IT GIVES US THE CONFIDENCE TO EXPECT GOD'S GLORIOUS WORKS IN OUR LIVES, TO SEE HOPE REALIZED AND DREAMS MANIFESTED.

Without Jesus, our sins would have been covered up but not forgiven. Without Jesus, we would not be heirs to the covenant of our forefather Abraham and we would not be partakers of the blessings. Without Jesus, we would not have access to the abundant life.

It is through Jesus, through faith in Jesus, that we are "reconciled to God and having been reconciled we are saved by His life" (Romans 5:10). It is through faith in Jesus and the shedding of His blood that we "receive God's sprit and are adopted as His own children. Now we call Him Abba, Father" (Romans 8:12). It is through faith in Jesus and the shedding of His blood that we are heirs to the Covenant of Abraham and "in fact, together with Christ we are heirs of God's glory"

(Romans 8:17). It is through faith in Jesus and the shedding of His blood that "we can boldly enter heaven's Most Holy Place" (Hebrew 10:19). It is through faith in Jesus and His blood that we have the "promise of eternal life" (1 John 2:25). It is through faith in Jesus and His blood that we have peace and are healed from every affliction, every aliment: "the chastisement for our peace was upon Him, and by His stripes we are healed" (Isaiah 53:5). It is through faith in Jesus and His blood that "both Gentiles and Jews who believe the Good News share equally in the riches inherited by God's children" and we are able to "enjoy the promise of blessings because we belong to Christ Jesus" (Ephesians 3:6).

Our faith begins and ends with our Lord and Savior, Jesus Christ. Jesus is the Lamb of God (John 1:36) and through Him we have full access to God. Our faith begins with the understanding that Jesus is the reason for the victories in our lives. It is our faith in Jesus that positions us to receive the supernatural blessings. It gives us the confidence to expect everyday miracles in our lives. It gives us the confidence to expect God's glorious works in our lives, to see hope realized and dreams manifested. It is our faith in Jesus that gives us the confidence to know that when we pray, God hears us, and everything we pray for will be given to us by Him, according to His will, through His son Jesus Christ. Knowing who we are through Christ, knowing what we can do through Christ, and knowing what we have through Christ make up the groundwork of everlasting faith. It is this relationship to Christ that activates the faithfulness of God. So what is faith?

Faith

"Faith is the substance of things hope for, the evidence of things not seen" (Hebrews 11:1). This may not be a new scripture to you—you've probably read it countless times, or heard it said "somewhere" by "someone" at "some point," but let's break it down a little bit.

> FAITH SEES THINGS HOPED FOR AS REALITY AND FAITH MAKES PLAINLY VISIBLE THE THINGS NOT SEEN.

The word "substance" means "essence" or the "physical reality or nature of a thing," and the word "evidence" means "proof" or "to make plainly visible." Therefore, we can conclude that faith sees things hoped for as *reality* and faith *makes plainly visible* the things not seen. In other words, faith does not wait to see to believe; faith believes and receives. So how does one develop faith? Through the Word of God.

"Faith comes by hearing, and hearing by the word of God" (Romans 10:17). Despite what you've been told, despite what the world says, true and sustainable faith is developed *only* through the Word—through hearing the Word on a consistent basis and receiving it within your heart as divine truth. This is why the speaking-life process is so essential. When we speak the Word of God, we hear it and it takes root in our hearts—and a heart filled with the Word is a heart filled with faith.

Without the Word of God, faith is baseless. Mediating on the Word, speaking it aloud, and allowing it to take residence in our hearts prepares us for times of battle. It prepares us to fight when our faith is tested. Faith and the Word will always go hand in hand—no Word, no faith.

Now, think about this: Do you truly have faith and do you trust God? When things aren't going according to plan, where is your faith—is it still going strong? When the winds of life are boisterous and contrary to your desired direction, are you still holding on to your faith? Do you trust God despite what you see?

FAITH VERSUS TRUST

In order to live victorious lives, we must examine the difference between "faith in God" and "trust in God." No, they are not the same. In fact, many times we have *faith* but lack *trust* in God. As a result, when things are not looking the way God promised us they would look, and our "faith juice" from last Sunday's service begins to wear off, we find ourselves entering into "let *me* figure it out" mode. We immediately put in place our back-up plans, our back-up back-up plans, our just-in-case plans, and our you-never-know plans. This, my friends, is a lack of trust in God. We've heard the Word, we know the Word, we believe the Word, but oftentimes we do not trust the process.

> FAITH REQUIRES HOPE IN THE UNSEEN, WHILE TRUST REQUIRES US TO NOT BE MOVED BY WHAT IS SEEN.

Faith is the foundation of hope, while trust is the building blocks upon which hope is realized. Faith requires hope in the unseen, while trust requires us to *not* be moved by what is seen. Faith says, "I know God hears my prayers, and He is able," while trust says, "But if things don't work the way I envisioned, I will not lose my joy, I will not waver. I still believe—His will be done and not mine." Trust is faith minus the back-up plan; it allows us to enter into divine rest and peace.

So often we say that we believe, but when life starts to unravel and prayers seem like they are not being answered, we begin to doubt God and lose faith. But, children of God, it is of the utmost importance that we transition from simple faith to trust in God.

Transitioning from Faith to Trust

Transitioning from faith to trust requires us to not be moved by our circumstances. It requires us to stand firm on the promises of God, regardless of what we see. We know we've made the transition when everything in our lives seems to be contrary to the visions and dreams that God has given us and yet, we have peace. That's trust! Trust requires us to relinquish control. It requires what I call the "white-flag mentality"—total surrender to God's will, vision, plan, and timing and not our own. It is "Lord, your will be done and not mine."

To trust God is to have full confidence in His Word. With trust the Word becomes "a lamp unto our feet and a light unto our paths" (Psalms 119:105). Trusting God means that no matter what happens, we believe and continue to believe. It is at this point we are "no longer leaning on our own understanding but instead allowing God to direct our paths" (Proverbs 3:5).

Trusting God is the point at which we look debt, death, sicknesses, disappointments, and a host of other trials and tribulations square in the eye and declare, "I shall not be moved by what I see. As I do what I am naturally able to do, my Father God is faithful to do His supernatural deeds, and He will deliver me from it all. He said it, I believe it, and it is so!" It is at this point that the Word of God and His promises to us are the solid rocks upon which our lives are built.

One of the greatest examples of faith and trust is the story of Shadrach, Meshach, and Abed-Nego. This scripture almost brought tears to my eyes the first time I read it, and I just kept reading it over and over again. If you recall, King Nebuchadnezzar commanded these three young men to bow down to his idol, threatened them with the fiery furnace, and challenged their God. But Shadrach, Meshach and Abed-Nego's responded, "O Nebuchadnezzar, we have no need to answer you in this matter. If that is the case, our God whom we serve is able to deliver us from the burning fiery furnace, and He will deliver us from your hand, O king. But if not, let it be known to you, O king, that we do

> FAITH MAY EXIST INDEPENDENTLY OF TRUST, BUT TRUST CANNOT EXIST IN THE ABSENCE OF FAITH—TRUST REQUIRES THE FOUNDATION OF FAITH.

not serve your gods, nor will we worship the gold image which you have set up" (Daniel 3:16-18). Now, we can clearly see from their response that these young men knew who their Father was and knew His character! I wonder, if faced with a similar situation today, how many of us would be so brave to stand up to a powerful king and boldly declare our confidence, faith, and trust in God, despite the threat of death?

Shadrach, Meshach, and Abed-Nego first expressed their faith in God by informing the king that their God "is able to deliver us…and He will," but they didn't leave it at that. No, they then transitioned their belief from simple faith to trust in God by saying, "But if not, let it be known to you, O king, that we do not serve your gods." This is a critical point. By simply saying "but," these three young men essentially surrendered to God's will and not their own. With the simple injection of the word "but," they proudly and unapologetically expressed unwavering faith and trust in God's will and His ways. Of course, in the end, God delivered them from the fiery furnace without even the smell of smoke on their garments. Take note that this is the God we serve—one who is just and faithful to deliver us from the all fiery furnaces of our lives, if we simply have faith and trust in Him.

> HOW WE REACT TO THE DISAPPOINTMENTS, FAILURES, AND TRAGEDIES IS A DIRECT REFLECTION OF THE DEPTH AND STRENGTH OF OUR FAITH AND THE FOUNDATION UPON WHICH OUR FAITH IS BUILT.

Faith may exist independently of trust, but trust cannot exist in the absence of faith—trust requires the foundation of faith. Faith and trust are the two necessary elements needed to build a house of victories, one that shall not fail or fall. The rains may descend, the floods may rise, the winds of life may beat violently against it, but it still stands. With faith and trust, the foundation is solid, blocks are securely laid down, and victory is imminent.

DEVELOPING YOUR FAITH AND TRUST

We must develop our faith and trust in God by renewing our minds with the Word of God and by believing the Word. We must take the Word for what it is and resist the temptation to second-guess the promises of God. This development process is a cumulation of everything we've discussed in previous pockets. It involves:

1. Knowing and believing that you are a child of the Most High God, heir to the covenant of our forefather Abraham, with blood-bought rights to go boldly and confidently to the throne of God, asking whatever you need and believing that as a Father, God is faithful to provide.

2. Renewing your mind with the Word of God. Taking every word, every promise for what it is, believing it, and allowing it to take residence in your heart.

3. Speaking life, speaking the Word of God over your life. "Calling those things which do not exist as though they did" (Romans 4:17)—prophesying over your life and

circumstances.

4. Not being moved by what you see with your natural eyes but instead expecting, believing, and patiently waiting for the manifestation of the promises. James 1:2-4 says: "Count it all joy when you fall into various trials, knowing that the testing of your faith produces patience. But let patience have its perfect work, that you may be perfect and complete, lacking nothing."

Having faith in God does not eliminate trials and tribulations in life. But, how we *react* to the disappointments, failures, and tragedies is a direct reflection of the depth and strength of our faith and the foundation upon which our faith is built.

Jesus reminds us in John 16:33 that "in the world you will have tribulation; but be of good cheer, I have overcome the world." Therefore, our faith must be rooted and grounded in Jesus Christ. It is through our faith in Christ that we have victory; it is in our faith in Christ that we are able to speak to unfavorable circumstances and watch them turn around. When we nurture and develop our faith in the Lord our God, failure is no longer an option. When we develop our faith in God, who is all-powerful and all-knowing, making Him and Him alone the foundation upon which we stand, we will truly see victories in all areas of our lives.

> THIS IS NOT YOUR TIME TO QUIT. THIS IS YOUR SEASON TO SOAR LIKE AN EAGLE. GRAB HOLD OF THE PROMISES OF GOD AND "FIGHT THE GOOD FIGHT OF FAITH".

"Jesus Christ is the same yesterday, today, and forever" (Hebrew 13:8). He is constant, true, and faithful. He never fails, and faith in Him will never fail us. Do not be discouraged or lose hope—there is nothing you cannot do through Christ. You may feel that you are in the "valley of the dry bones," so to speak, and everything around you may seem dead—dead dreams and a dismal future. But, this is the time to ask yourself, can God breathe life into this seemingly dead future? Your answer should be a resounding "Yes!" This is not your time to quit. This is your season to soar like an eagle. Grab hold of the promises of God and "fight the good fight of faith" (1 Timothy 6:12). Have faith and trust in God for all the victories of your life.

CHILDLIKE FAITH

As children of God, we must "receive the kingdom of God as a little child" (Mark 10:15). This requires us to throw intellect and logic out the window as it pertains to God, the Kingdom of God, and His promises. This, I know, may be difficult for many of us—we are intellectuals, taught to always question things and find logical patterns, but "God is the supreme God of the heavens above and the earth below" (Joshua 2:11 NLT). There is no rationalizing Him and His works. He is unfathomable and indescribable. And if we are ever to see the manifestations of His promises in our lives, we must have childlike faith.

Think for a moment about the characteristics of little children: They are innocent; they see things through eager eyes; they are easily amazed; they are dependent upon their parents; they are sincere; they are trusting and God forbid you make them a promise—they will never let you off the hook! Seriously, have you ever made a promise to a child? Months or even years may pass, yet every time you are in that child's presence, he or she will remind you of the promise: "Remember you promised me that you were going to...." That's a child! And that's how we need to approach God as His children—trusting in Him, relying completely on Him, believing His promises, reminding Him of His promises, and expecting the manifestations of the promises even after much time has passed.

This is not the season to give up or to lose faith. God is your heavenly Father and Jesus is your heavenly Brother, Savior and Friend—all power is in His hands and He has everything you need. You may not see it yet, but faith is believing that you will one day see it. If you saw what you hoped for immediately, then there would be no need to hope—for "hope that is seen is no hope at all. Who hopes for what he already has?" (Romans 8:24 NIV). Faith is believing that God is able, and that He will follow through on His promises. Believe every promise He has made to you; believe His Word. Resist the temptation to question through lack of faith. Instead, like a child, simply believe.

> TOO OFTEN WE ARE BLINDED BY OUR DESIRES AND FAIL TO SEEK GOD FOR HIS.

Surrendering to His Desires

As we continue on this faith journey, we must understand that our lives will dramatically change for the better when we surrender to God's desires for our lives—for every area, every person, and every situation in our lives. Too often we are blinded by our desires and fail to seek God for His. We want what we want, when we want it, and when we don't get it, our faith falters. But as believers, we must entrust our lives to God, seeking His desires for every area of our lives.

For many years, prior to my life with Christ, whenever I prayed I would always find it so difficult to say, "God, if it is Your will, let it be." It was virtually impossible to get these words out of my mouth. If I were superman, these words would have been my kryptonite—I feared them! Why? Because I thought, "What if God does not want what I want?" The thought of God not wanting what I so desperately wanted for myself crippled me with fear. After all, how could God not want me to have handsome Russell? Granted, he has a checkered past, dark secrets, and a twisted personality that I am completely oblivious to—"but he has a beautiful smile and I love him," I would think. "I know He's the one, and asking God if it's His will would only complicate things for me." So, as if God were not aware of my thoughts, I would quickly mumble the words or just omit them altogether, thinking

> THERE IS NO IMPERFECTION IN GOD'S TIMING. HE IS AN EXTRAORDINARY GOD WHO HAS EXTRAORDINARY PLANS FOR OUR LIVES.

somehow that I was tricking God into giving me what I wanted. In retrospect, how sadly deceived was I!

I am so thankful that God ignored many of my "emotional" pleas and did not submit to *my* will. Today my prayers are laced with "God, Your will be done and not mine." I've learned that God's desires for my life will always exceed my desires for my own life, and His desires will always produce victories.

Entrusting one's life to God means we have transitioned from faith to trust—trusting that He has our best in His hands. It is trusting that if we don't see our desired outcome, then God has a better plan for us. It is complete confidence in God, knowing and believing that no matter what comes our way, "all things work together for our good" because we love Him and are called according to His purpose (Romans 8:28).

As we develop our faith and trust, we must be willing to give God control over our lives. He is the divine orchestrator. He opens and closes doors at the right times. He puts the right people in our paths and removes the wrong ones at the right time. He blesses us with the right opportunities at the right time. He orchestrates "chance" encounters at the right time. There is no imperfection in God's timing. He is an extraordinary God who has extraordinary plans for our lives. That's Abba, our Father—His desires for our lives will always put our desires to shame, and surrendering to His desires opens the floodgates to an abundance of blessings.

Faith, Not Emotions

Now, in life there are many things we have to face. We all have experienced some situations that left us scratching our headings wondering what went wrong. There are many battles we have to fight on a daily basis and most, if not all of us, wish we could buy a one-way ticket to Easy Ville—where life is easy and the living is sweet! Cheesy? Maybe. But, if we are honest with ourselves, many of us will admit that from time to time we fantasize about the good old days— the days before the job that we dread going to on a daily basis; before the children and spouses; before the endless bills and all the responsibilities of life. Looking at our lives today, it may seem as if it's spiraling out of control. We are always on the go; we barely have any time for ourselves. And, God forbid something does not go according to plan, then it seems that everything we perceive to be wrong in our lives is suddenly magnified.

> GOD IS MOVED BY OUR FAITH, NOT OUR EMOTIONS.

This then gives us an opportunity to throw ourselves a pity party—a one-guest soiree to the dullest party in town, where the theme is self-pity, the mood is depression, the attitude is self-doubt, and the dress code is pajamas, a tee, socks (optional), and a blanket. There is no fun at this soiree—in fact, we barely make it out of bed. We sulk all day, eat all day, and entertain floods of negative thoughts and emotions all day. At this party, we sit and wish that things ran a little smoother in our lives and that we weren't so stressed all the time. We wish the children would do as they are told, the minute they are told. We wish our spouses would help a little bit more or be more affectionate. We wish friends wouldn't betray us and family members would support us. We wish we didn't have to feel the pain of a relationship gone wrong. We wish, we wish, and we wish some more. And when we are not wishing, we are praying, pleading, crying, and praying some more. But, here's the thing—God is not moved by our emotions. I can hear the gasps now: "Really?!" Yes, really.

God is compassionate and merciful, but crying all day long, being angry with God, and threatening Him does not motivate Him to work on our behalf. God is moved by our faith, not our emotions. Unfortunately, sometimes we think that if we cry long enough, if we pray long enough, if we plead long enough, God will act on our behalf. But faith is what pleases God (Hebrew 11:6), and this has never been more evident than in Jesus's ministry here on earth.

If we look closely at Jesus's healing and deliverance ministry, we will notice that it was most often accompanied with the affirmation of faith. Jesus said to the sinful woman, "*Your faith* has saved you. Go in peace" (Luke 7:50), and when approached by two blind men His response was, "Do you believe that I am able to do this?" They said to Him, "Yes, Lord." Then He touched their eyes, saying, "According to *your faith* let it be to you" (Matthew 9:28-29). In Luke 17:19, when Jesus was approached by ten lepers, He said, "Arise, go your way. *Your faith* has made you well." When the blind man shouted out to Jesus to have mercy upon him, His response was, "Receive your sight; *your faith* has made you well" (Luke 18:42). And let's not forget about the woman with the issue of blood! Jesus's response to this desperate woman was, "Daughter, be of good cheer; *your faith* has made you well. Go in peace" (Luke 8:48). This is the goodness of our Lord God, one whose "righteousness is revealed from faith to faith; as it is written, *'The just shall live by faith.'"* (Romans 1:17).

> INCREASING FAITH PLUS DECREASING EMOTIONS EQUALS INFINITE POSSIBILITIES AND SURPASSING VICTORIES.

God acts on our behalf according to our faith, not according to our emotions. Doubt, fear, and unbelief are blessing blockers, as is written in Matthew 13:58: "He did not do many mighty works there because of their unbelief." Therefore, this is not the time in your life, child of God, to be ruled by emotions—this is your season to see God's glorious works revealed in your life!

Yes, it is okay to cry. Yes, it is okay to sulk for a bit. Yes, it is okay to be angry. Emotions are a natural attribute of the human character. But, after you are through crying, after you have vented and gotten it all out, know that God's magnificent blessings are there waiting for you to receive them—but only through your faith. Lift your head, stand tall, and believe. Increasing faith plus decreasing emotions equals infinite possibilities and surpassing victories.

Delays Do Not Always Mean "No!"

Delays are a natural part of life, but "perceived" delays do not necessarily mean that God is saying no to our prayers. Like any loving father who has our best interest at heart, God loves us so much that He may not give us what we ask for when we ask for it. We must let go of the notion that things should go according to "our plan," because in fact, "a day is like a thousand years to the Lord, and a thousand years is like a day" (2 Peter 3:8). Our plans may not be God's plan, and God's timing may not necessarily coincide with our planned timing. Therefore, when you've prayed and prayed and prayed and still it seems that nothing is happening, it may be the result of one of five things:

> HE SITS HIGH ABOVE AND HE HAS FULL VIEW OF OUR PAST, OUR PRESENT, AND OUR FUTURE. WHEN WE THINK WE ARE READY, GOD SEES AHEAD AND KNOWS THAT WE ARE NOT READY.

1. There may be areas of disobedience, unforgivingness, and/or strife that need to be dealt with. This is not to say that we must be perfect in order to receive the blessings of God, for as much as sin exists, grace abounds (Romans 5:20). But as previously mentioned, there are consequences to disobedience. Think back to the children of Israel, how they wandered in the wilderness for forty years before reaching the promised land. A journey which should have taken them eleven days took forty years (Deuteronomy 1:2-3) due to disobedience, murmuring,

and strife. God is always there for us, but by our own actions, we may unknowingly block the work of His hands in our lives. It may be something that was said or not said, something that was done or not done. Whatever it is, we must address it, repent, and reestablish our proper standing with God.

2. Our requests may simply not be in line with God's desires for our lives. It is important that our prayers and requests are aligned with the Word of God and His desires for our lives. We limit God when we only want what we want for ourselves. 1 John 5:14-15 says, "If we ask anything according to *His will*, He hears us. And if we know that He hears us, whatever we ask, we know that we have the petitions that we have asked of Him." As previously mentioned, it is imperative to seek God for His will and His desires for our lives, because His desires are far greater than our desires could ever be for our own lives. (See Pocket 7: Super Enabler.)

3. It may not be the right time. All throughout the bible are references to a "due season" or "due time." The word "due" refers to an "appointed time" or an "expected time." Psalm 145:15 says, "The eyes of all look expectantly to You, and You give them their food in due season," and Habakkuk 2:3 says, "For the vision is yet for an appointed time; but at the end it will speak, and it will not lie. Though it tarries, wait for it; because it will surely come, it will not tarry." God knows His plans for us and everything works according to His plan and purpose. He is a

God of seasons, and oftentimes our blessings are directly related to the blessings of another individual or persons. In other words, God blesses us so that we may be a blessing, and everything is orchestrated so that His will is done and purposes fulfilled at the appointed time.

4. God uses the in-between times as a test of our faith. 1 Peter 1:6-7 tells us that "there is wonderful joy ahead, even though you have to endure many trials for a little while. These trials will show that your faith is genuine. It is being tested as fire tests and purifies gold—though your faith is far more precious than mere gold," and in Jeremiah 17:10, God says, "I, the Lord, search the heart, I test the mind." God is interested in our true motives—what's truly in our hearts and what motivates our desires. It is one thing to praise God when all is going well, but it's an entirely different thing to still have praise in your heart when nothing is going your way. It is therefore important to perform a "heart check" from time to time. Why do we want what we want, and what happens if we don't get it when we want it, or don't receive it at all? God wants to know if our love for Him is genuine or if it is tied up to "things," or what we think we can get from Him. If He took it all away, would we still love Him? These are issues of our hearts that God wants to bring to light. God is omniscient—He already knows what's in our hearts, but the purpose of testing is to expose our hearts to the Light, and it is His hope that this exposure leads us to repentance.

5. We may simply not be ready for the manifestation of the promises. Our dreams and our successes may seem delayed because, frankly, we may not be spiritually mature enough to handle the consequences of success. Now, this is not to say that success will not come, but it means that God has some character building to do, and it is within those "valley moments" that He molds us and strengthens us for the blessings ahead. "The Lord isn't really being slow about his promise, as some people think. No, he is being patient for your sake" (2 Peter 3:9). God sees our weaknesses when we don't see them. He sits high above and He has full view of our past, our present, and our future. When we think we are ready, God sees ahead and knows that we are not ready. He knows that if he gives some of us what we ask for this minute, we would soon enough forget that He was the source of the blessings. He knows that many of us would have egos as big as our heads. We would write books and produce movies about how "we made it." We would exclaim, "Look what *I* did! Look what *I* accomplished!" And He would cease to get the glory from our lives. Now, some folks may shake their heads and say, "No, not me!," but God knows you more than you know yourself, and He is preparing you mentally, spiritually, emotionally, and physically for all that He has in store for you. This way, He alone gets the glory.

Oftentimes we don't recognize that there is a process involved that takes us from where we are, to where God wants us to be. We don't recognize the long, tedious road that we must travel from the dreams and visions to the manifestation of the promises in our lives. On this journey there may be bumps, roadblocks, potholes, and sometimes even road erosion along the way. The ride will not be smooth, but when we give God the wheel, He is faithful to safely deliver us to our predestined destinations.

> THIS IS THE TYPE OF FAITH WE MUST ALL STRIVE TO HAVE—ABRAHAMIC FAITH. FAITH THAT WITHSTANDS THE TEST OF TIME AND HOLDS UP REGARDLESS OF TIME.

Consider Abraham for a moment. He was seventy-five years of age when God promised to make him a father of many, but it was twenty-five years *later*, when Abraham was a hundred years old, that Isaac, the son God promised, was born. Now, I know most of you may be thinking, "But I don't want to wait twenty-five years for the blessings! I want them now!" Again, God's timing is not our timing, but His timing is perfect. We must begin to trust God, to trust His timing for our lives and not our own.

Romans 4:19-21 says that Abraham "not being weak in faith, did not consider his own body, already dead (since he was about a hundred years old), and the deadness of Sarah's womb. He did not waver at the promise of God through unbelief, but was strengthened in faith, giving glory to God and being fully convinced that what He had promised He was also able to perform." Abraham was not affected by what He saw in the natural realm. He knew enough about God—about His character and faithfulness—to know that God would do what

He said He would do, even if it seemed impossible to the natural eye, even if it seemed that the blessings were delayed. This is the type of faith we must all strive to have—Abrahamic faith. Faith that withstands the test of time and holds up regardless of time. Faith that says, "Lord, you said it; I believe it is so and I expect it. Your will be done and not mine in Jesus's name."

GOD, NOT THINGS

As we grow from faith to faith, it is important to make sure that our faith remains grounded in God. Why? Because life presents us with so many opportunities, and if we are not careful, we may sometimes mistakenly place our faith in things other than God. If we are not careful, we may place our faith in our physical abilities, strengths, capabilities, people and objects. If we are not careful, we may knowingly or unknowingly start believing that it is our elite education that open doors for us, that it is our impressive professional experiences that guarantee us that dream job or promotion, that it is our charm that wins us friends, that it is our money that have us living privileged lifestyles, that it is our connections that seal the deal. If we are not careful, we may start having faith in people, circumstances, and things. And when all these fail, our lives are ruined, our hopes are

> YOUR LEVEL OF PREPARATION, MOTIVATION, AND DRIVE IS EQUIVALENT TO YOUR LEVEL OF FAITH.

dashed, and our dreams are crushed.

Now, let me clarify: I am in no way saying that one should not be prepared, that one should not strive for excellence in one's professional and personal life. Quite the contrary. In fact, your level of preparation, motivation, and drive is equivalent to your level of faith. Therefore, I encourage you to prepare for your blessings—get your education, plan your future, and make your connections. But, at the end of the day, your faith must be based in God, for "He is the one who gives us power to get wealth; to be successful" (Deuteronomy 8:18). It is through His grace that we have what we have, and will be blessed with more.

"Have faith in God" (Mark 11:22) and keep your faith grounded in Him alone. It is not God's desire for us to put our faith in anything or anyone except Him. Jesus tells us in Mark 11:22-23 that our faith in God empowers us to move mountains. Note that He did not say, "Have faith that your strength will move mountains" or "Have faith that you can telepathically move mountains." He simply said, "Have faith in God."

Visualize that for a moment: Your faith in God can move mountains! Your mountain may be debt, sickness, addiction, depression, unemployment—anything that seems like a barrier. It is insurmountable, and you just can't seem to get past it or over it—except through faith in God.

When we exercise our faith in God regarding all things and all areas of our lives, it pleases Him, for "without faith it is impossible to please God, for he who comes to God must believe that He is, and that He is a rewarder of those who diligently seek Him" (Hebrew 11:6). Our faith in Him gives Him the opportunity to open supernatural doors in our lives. It gives Him the opportunity to open doors to amazing blessings and perform astonishing miracles in our lives. It is therefore paramount that we, as believers, take inventory of our faith, consistently monitoring the levels of our faith and making sure that the foundations of such faith is in God and God alone.

Faith, Action, and Rest

Faith, in some situations, propels us into action. It requires us to be active participants in the process. In cases like these, faith is not hoping and praying without action. It is not wishing upon a lucky star, sitting back and expecting God to work. In these situations, faith and works go hand in hand, "for as the body without the spirit is dead, so faith without works is dead also" (James 2:26). The steps or actions we take are reflections of our faith.

> IF WE ARE NOT CAREFUL, WE WILL RUN OURSELVES INTO THE GROUND TRYING TO "FIX," "CHANGE," AND "SAVE." THESE ARE THE CIRCUMSTANCES THAT REQUIRE US TO ENTER INTO "SURRENDERING REST."

If, for instance, you have prayed to get out of debt, and believe that God wants you to prosper in all things, if you have faith in Him but are not taking the necessary actions to get out of debt, then your faith is null and void. If you have faith for a new job but haven't applied to any positions since 1993, your faith is null and void. If you have faith in God for a house but haven't taken the appropriate steps to purchase that house, your faith is null and void. In circumstances like these, true faith leads to visions, plans, and actions. "By works faith is made perfect" (James 2:22), and with faith there is nothing we cannot do, no dream we cannot make a reality, no goal we cannot accomplish.

Faith may propel us into action sometimes but, other times, faith is characterized by rest. This rest is *not* a lazy rest. It is not an "I don't want to do anything. I'm just going sit here and wait for God to drop the blessings from the sky" sort of a rest. No, that's just laziness! This rest frees us from worry and anxiety. This is "surrendering rest." It's when you've done everything in your power to change a situation, but have realized that you don't have the power to change it, so you surrender to the authority and power of Jesus Christ.

The fact is there are just some things we can't do. There are just some things that God has to do for us, and He does not need our assistance to do it. In these circumstances, our "assistance" serves more as a hindrance, blocking the works of God. For instance, you may have a loved one whom you are trying to "fix," "change," "save," or all of the above. You have enthusiastically applied the scripture "faith without works is dead," so you are on a mission to "fix, change, and save" this individual. You formulate a plan: Feed them the scripture daily, convince them that they are "sinners" and need to change, give them the old guilt trip, trick them into going to church or at least watching a television sermon. You try and try, you toil and toil, but it just seems like your loved one is even more defiant, and you are now out of tactics. This is because in situations like this, faith requires rest. Faith says, "You don't have the power to fix, change, or save anyone, not even yourself!"

> IF YOU REALLY DESIRE TO SEE THE MANIFESTATIONS OF VICTORIES IN YOUR LIFE, HERE'S THE THING YOU MUST DO—YOU MUST SIMPLY BELIEVE AND HOLD ON.

Our missions to "save" are fueled by our love for others. But oftentimes, if we are not careful, we will run ourselves into the ground trying to "fix," "change," and "save." These are the circumstances that require us to enter into "surrendering rest." This is the point when we cease from "works"—we've done all we can possibly do and now we surrender it up to God through prayers—trusting and having faith in Him, believing that He is faithful to deliver and save through our Lord and Savior, Jesus Christ.

Now, your situation may not be related to the salvation of a loved one. You may have exhausted all possibilities in a particular situation, and now your faith requires that you surrender and rest. In any case, whether we work or rest, our faith will always yield victories. Trust, believe, and have faith!

HOLDING ON TO FAITH AND TRUST

Regardless of what we may face in life, it is important

that we hold on to our faith and trust in God, believing His promises to us and expecting the manifestations in our lives. Now, you may think, "Well, life just isn't looking too promising right now," and I understand—life may be difficult sometimes. You may have had "plans," you may have thought that you would have been married at this stage in your life, or at least found "the one." You may have thought that you would have had the career you wanted by now, the house, the car, the money, and all that comes with success, but nothing is what you thought it would be. Where you are at this point in your life is not where you believe you should be—you believe that your life is way behind schedule and you just don't know how to catch up at this point. I understand—I was there.

Many of you may even feel that God has made some promises to you and broken them. He may have given you visions, dreams and even sent a prophet or two with a word of encouragement just when you needed it most. He may have spoken to you about your future blessings: your spouse, your ministries, your anointing, your new levels and new territories—but nothing in the natural realm seems to be in alignment with His promises. In fact, it has been years since the visions, dreams, and prophets, and there are still no visible manifestations in your life. It may seem that every time you take one step forward, you end up taking ten steps back, and you just can't seem to get ahead. You may be losing hope and doubt may be creeping in: "I don't think this is this ever going to happen for me." But, child of God, hold on to your faith and trust God! If you really desire to see the manifestations of victories in your life, here's the thing you must do—

you must simply believe and hold on.

Holding on to faith is holding on to the Word of God. Building your faith through the Word of God "is like a man building a house, who dug deep and laid the foundation on the rock. And when the flood arose, the stream beat vehemently against that house, and could not shake it, for it was founded on the rock" (Luke 6:48). The Word is our rock, and this is the time when we must not give up! We must speak life over our situations and engage the sword—the Word of God—and expect victories. The Word of God is what we need for every battle, and belief in His Word is what we need to live victoriously.

> DO. NOT. GIVE. UP! YOUR BLESSINGS AND BREAKTHROUGHS ARE JUST AHEAD. HAVE FAITH, HOLD ON, AND TRUST GOD.

When our lives are in shambles and prayers seem to be falling on deaf ears, we must believe the Word when it says, "Whatever things you ask when you pray, believe that you receive them, and you will have them" (Mark 11:24). We must believe it when it says, "Whatever you ask the Father in My name [Jesus's name] He will give you" (John 16:23). And we must believe it when it says, "Ask, and it will be given to you; seek, and you will find; knock, and it will be opened to you" (Luke 11:9). We must hold on to the Word of God which says, "Those who seek the Lord shall not lack any good thing" (Psalm 34:10). When it seems that we are being attacked at every turn, we must trust in the Word, which says, "If you make the LORD your refuge; if you make the Most High your shelter, no evil will conquer you; no plague will come near your home. For he will order his angels to protect you wherever you go" (Psalm 91:9-11). God's words are His promises to us and the grounds for our faith.

Have faith that you "will live and not die" (Psalm 118:17). Have faith that your children will not stumble, despite what you see, because the Word of God says, "Train up a child up in the way he should go, and when he is old, he shall not depart" (Proverbs 22:6). Have faith for your breakthrough, have faith for your healing, have faith for your deliverance, have faith for your finances, have faith for your children, have faith for your spouse, have faith for your prosperity, have faith for your blessings. Have faith, have faith, have faith!

God has so many blessings in store for us. His blessings are not only for the "next" guy; they are for each and every one of us. The good life is not only for our neighbors—the good life also has our names on it! But, we must believe and resist the temptation to give up. Do. Not. Give. Up! Your blessings and breakthroughs are just ahead. Have faith, hold on, and trust God.

So often we throw in the towel just before the promises are fulfilled. We give up on our dreams, we dismiss the visions, we think, "Yeah, good for him, but I'm not that lucky." We make excuses why it's never going to happen, casually exclaiming, "I just don't have the money" or "I don't have the connections" or "I'm just not smart enough." We throw in the old cop-out statement "I'm okay; not everyone was meant to have that," knowing that our souls are screaming, "I want that!" We start doubting ourselves: "What was I thinking? That could never be me. I could never have that!" and questioning if we really heard from God: "Maybe I didn't hear Him well; maybe that's not what He said." When everyone around us seems to be prospering in all areas of their lives, we start believing that God loves the next person more than He loves us. We are not able to see past the chaos, disappointments, and difficult times. At this point we give up, resolving to simply exist and not live. But as believers, new and not so new, we must hold on, have faith, and trust God. "God is not a man, so he does not lie. He is not human, so he does not change his mind" (Numbers 23:19 NLT).

> EVERY STRUGGLE IS AN OPPORTUNITY TO GROW AND DEVELOP OUR FAITH AND TRUST IN HIM.

There is nothing that God has spoken that He shall fail to act on, or promised that He shall not make good on. If He said it, it shall be. If He promised it, it shall be. Everything He has spoken into your life, every promise He has made to you, He is faithful to deliver—but you must have faith and trust that God wants the best for you. Despite where you are in your life today, despite what you see, believe God, trust His word, and hold on to your faith. You may not be where you would like to be, the promises may seem delayed, but I encourage you to walk by faith and not by sight. Do not be swayed, or discouraged by what you see. Have faith!

God uses every struggle to teach us, and if we just stop

for a moment—stop complaining just for a second—we will be able to see His glorious works manifested in our lives in the most magnificent ways. Every struggle is an opportunity to grow and develop our faith and trust in Him. Every trial is an opportunity to be drawn into a deeper, more committed relationship with our Lord and Savior, Jesus Christ. Do not be shaken by the trials of life, or be moved by what you see in the natural realm. Be encouraged, inspired, and motivated by the supernatural powers of God. Keep your eyes fixated on Christ; believe that "what's impossible with man is possible with God" (Luke 18:27). Have faith, trust, and believe that with God on your side, the best is truly yet to come. Remember: "If you can believe, all things are possible to him who believes" (Mark 9:23). Believe and receive your victories in Jesus's Name!

MAKE YOUR OWN NOTES

Do you trust and have faith in God despite your circumstances?

> "FAITH IS THE SUBSTANCE OF THINGS HOPE FOR, THE EVIDENCE OF THINGS NOT SEEN."
>
> ~ HEBREW 11:1

POCKET 7

SUPER ENABLER

TANEKI DACRES

Always one to have big ideas, I was constantly trying to find my place in this world, a place where I could leave my mark. Unfortunately, while on this quest, I experienced firsthand what it means to be outside of God's will and purpose, and having to work three times as hard to make something happen in the flesh.

A few years back, after I sold the fast-food franchise, I had another "big" idea: to create a social-networking site with a business directory, part of which would promote the hottest clubs, lounges, and parties. "Clubs, lounges, and parties?!" you're saying. Yeah, let's just say that back then Jesus and I were neighbors but not friends just yet. Anyway, at the time I believed it was a great idea, and I was motivated. In those days there were very few social-networking sites that also offered business directories and city guides. I believed that I was in the position to truly succeed. So with my web-design experience, coupled with my programming knowledge and skills, I took on the ambitious task of building the site—I figured I'd put my bachelor's in computer information systems to good use. Plus, building the site myself allowed me to save tons of money on the cost of site development.

> WHERE THERE IS GOD'S PURPOSE, HIS WILL, AND OUR OBEDIENCE, WE WILL ALWAYS FIND THE EFFECTIVE POWER OF THE HOLY SPIRIT.

Long story short: What should have taken months to a year max to develop, test, and implement took years. By the launch date, I had tons of competitors. Now, I'm no tech genius, but I have some technical skills and, even if I don't know a programming language that well, I'm able to catch on pretty easily. But, not in this case. What should have been easy to me all of a sudden seemed complicated and I found myself struggling to figure out some of the simplest things. It seemed that with this venture there was an invisible roadblock and there was no way I was getting around it. Why? Because what I now know is, although this was a "great" idea, I was operating outside of God's purpose for my life. Therefore, I was not anointed for this venture.

The result of being outside of the will and purpose of God, outside of His anointing, was years of trials and failure, years of going in circles, "trying to make things happen" for myself. I never once stopped to ask God if any of these "bright" ideas were His purpose for my life. I just figured that I had a great idea and *I* was going to make it happen. There was no seeking, fasting and praying for direction. It was just me, my bright ideas, and my desire to make them work. I was motivated, I wasn't afraid of working hard, but I was not anointed. And where there is no anointing, there are unnecessary struggles, unnecessary trials which ultimately lead to unnecessary disappointments.

Shortly after the social-networking site failed—when Jesus and I finally became friends—I was able to successfully develop and design a website with minimal effort using the same programming language and software. Why? Because it was God's purpose for my life and so I had His anointing. This time was not like all the others. No, this time I had prayed and sought God for confirmation. He confirmed and, to my amazement, the anointing flowed like a river. Everything that had baffled me, everything that made me want to pull my hair out by the roots years ago, suddenly became clear and easy. The Holy Spirit took charge and gave me divine wisdom, knowledge, and understanding. He revealed ways to get over humps and bumps along the way and led me victoriously throughout the entire process.

> YOU ARE ANOINTED. YES, YOU–YOU ARE ANOINTED! YOU ARE CALLED, YOU HAVE PURPOSE, AND THERE IS GREATNESS LIVING INSIDE OF YOU.

In retrospect, I realize that it may have been God's will for me to design and develop a website—but not for the purpose of glorifying a lifestyle that is not pleasing to Him. What I had to learn was: where there is God's purpose, His will, and our obedience, we will always find the effective power of the Holy Spirit—the great, glorious anointing that empowers us to do what we may not otherwise have been able to do, and enables us to experience countless victories in everything that we do.

Called and Anointed

So, here you are, child of God. You know who you are and whose you are; you've let go of all the baggage from your past; you are renewing your mind daily; you're slowly but surely speaking life; you're trying to walk in the Spirit daily; and your faith and trust have grown tremendously. You are definitely not the person you used to be. You don't act the way you used to; you don't talk the way you used to; you don't go the places you used to; and you don't even spend time with the folks you used to. Everything in your life is new and fresh. Now you're trying to find your place in God's divine plan. You don't want to just exist—you want to live a victoriously fulfilling life. This is a new journey, a new adventure, and you're trying to find the right path. "What career should I pursue? What business should I embark on? What's my calling? What's my purpose? Where should I serve?" These are but a few of the questions you are beginning to ask yourself.

Well, if you are anything like I was, you may have heard of the "anointing," but you're not sure what it even means. You may have heard countless preachers talk about the "anointing," but they may as well have been speaking a foreign language, because you simply could not comprehend the concept. Or, you may be familiar with the "anointing"—you may have an understanding of it, but still not be sure how it can truly impact your life. Or, you may not be familiar with the word at all—this may be a completely new concept to you. Whatever the case, I'm here to tell you, child of God, that you are anointed. Yes, you—you are anointed! You are called, you have purpose, and there is greatness living inside you.

It took me a while to truly understand what it means to be anointed—and being the disciple that I am, I must admit that I'm still learning. The first time I ever had the word spoken directly to me and about me was by the stranger in the New York City train station on that very bleak day years ago.

Her exact words were, "You are anointed," and my thought was, "What does that mean?" I mean, sure, I had heard preachers talk about being "anointed," but what did that really mean to me? How did I become anointed and what does it mean to be anointed? For me, it took several years—through ups and downs, sickness and pain—before I had any real comprehension of what it meant to be anointed. Today, I can confidently say, "I am anointed." And so are you!

The Anointing

The word "anoint" means to "smear on" or "rub on," and the tradition of "anointing one with oil" can be found all throughout biblical history. From the Old Testament to the New Testament, things and people were anointed—set aside for the will and purpose of God. Kings were anointed: "And they anointed David king over Israel, according to the word of the lord by Samuel" (1 Chronicles 11:3). Priests were anointed: "And you shall anoint Aaron and his sons, and consecrate them, that they may minister to Me as priests" (Exodus 30:30). Objects were anointed for sanctification: "And you shall take the anointing oil, and anoint the tabernacle and all that is in it and you shall hallow it and all its utensils, and it shall be holy" (Exodus 40:9). Prophets were anointed: "And Elisha the son of Shaphat of Abel Me-

> WE ARE GOD'S CHOSEN CHILDREN, ANOINTED BY THE INDWELLING OF THE HOLY SPIRIT AND EMPOWERED TO ACCOMPLISH GOD'S WILL AND PURPOSES ON EARTH.

holah, you shall anoint as prophet in your place" (1 King 19:16). The sick were anointed for healing: "Anointed with oil many who were sick, and healed them" (Mark 6:13). But, the ultimate anointing was upon the Anointed One, the Messiah, our Lord and Savior, Jesus Christ: "God anointed Jesus of Nazareth with the Holy Spirit and with power, who went about doing good and healing all who were oppressed by the devil, for God was with Him" (Acts 10:38).

So, what's God's anointing? The anointing is God's supernatural oil or unction "smeared on" the lives of believers, enabling, authorizing, and empowering us for a particular task or purpose. It is God's supernatural on our natural—God's supernatural power, knowledge, and abilities rubbed onto our natural knowledge and abilities. The anointing is the supernatural work of the Holy Spirit—the Helper—authorizing and equipping us to do what we would not be able to successfully do on our own. It is God working in us and through us; we are the conduit by which He accomplishes His purposes.

In John 14:26, Jesus promises us "the Helper—the Holy Spirit, whom the Father will send in My name, He will teach you all things," and in Acts 1:8 Jesus says, "You shall receive power when the Holy Spirit has come upon you." This is the source by which our anointing flows. As children of God, "baptized with the Holy Spirit" (Acts 11:16), we are all anointed, for we "have an anointing from the Holy One" (1 John 2:20). Unlike in the days of the Old Testament, today—thanks to the work of our Savior, Jesus Christ, on the cross—we no longer need to have anyone anoint us with oil as a symbol of being chosen by God. No. Today we are joined to Christ, the Anointed One, and as a result are partakers of His anointing through the Holy Spirit. We are God's chosen children, anointed by the indwelling of the Holy Spirit and empowered to accomplish God's will and purposes on earth.

Experiencing the Anointing

It is an awesome thing to have readily available to us the power of the Almighty—to be empowered by God's supernatural power. No other religious or spiritual group can claim the anointing of God and see the tangible evidence of this anointing except for those who are saved by our Lord, Jesus Christ. The anointing is such a blessing to us, and although we may be motivated, excited, and ready to experience this awesome power, there is just one thing we need to do beforehand. To experience the anointing, we must first find God's specific will and purpose for our lives or for a particular situation.

> THE POWER OF GOD WILL BE MADE FULLY AVAILABLE TO US WHEN WE ARE IN HIS WILL AND HIS PURPOSE, AND WHEN WE ARE OBEDIENT TO THE HOLY SPIRIT.

We know that as born-again believers, as disciples of Christ, it is God's will for us to be "salt of the earth, and light of this world" (Matthew 5:13-14). It is His will for us to establish ministries, spreading the Good News of Jesus Christ. It is His will for us to intercede for others through prayer, to love others, to make disciples. We are called to serve and so much more. But to experience His anointing, we need to know how to go about doing and being what God has called us to do and be. The power of God will be made fully available to us when we are in His will and His purpose, and when we are obedient to the Holy Spirit.

God's purpose will determine the flow and visible evidence of the anointing. When we are "called according to His purpose," we know that "all things work together for good" (Romans 8:28). The effective power of the Holy Spirit will work together with our natural abilities to accomplish His purpose. The place where we find His purpose is the place where we find fulfillment in life.

God's will also determines the visible evidence of the anointing in our lives—"He does according to His will in the army of heaven and among the inhabitants of the earth" (Daniel 4:35). We are all uniquely anointed. We are all *not* called to be preachers on the pulpit. But, at the core of God's will, the anointing will always be for the benefit, the uplifting, the promotion, and the growth of the Kingdom of Heaven.

The anointing will not be effective if what we are embarking on is outside of God's will or purpose for our lives. "You can make many plans, but the LORD's purpose will prevail" (Proverbs 19:21 NLT). It is therefore imperative that we seek God's specific will and purpose for our lives in Christ. We must develop the habit of asking for God's will for all areas of our lives—making sure to include Him in all our decision-making processes. The place in life where we find His will is the place where we will experience an abundance of His anointing.

God's will and His purpose are interwoven but distinct: His will is the specific means or avenue by which we accomplish His purpose, while His purpose is His desired outcome. In other words, His will is the "how" and His purpose is the "why." For example, it may be God's will for you to embark on a business venture, but it may not be His purpose for you to embark on a business venture that involves taking advantage of the less fortunate. God is a God of purpose, and His anointing will always flow when the assignment or task is in alignment with His will and purpose.

> AS WE EMBARK ON THIS JOURNEY, WE MUST RESIST THE TEMPTATION TO WALK IN ANOTHER PERSON'S ANOINTING—WE MUST BE CONFIDENT IN KNOWING THAT OUR ANOINTING IS UNIQUE TO US.

Obedience to the direction of the Holy Spirit also determines the evidence of the anointing in our lives. The Holy Spirit gives us dreams, visions and speaks to us about our calling. But, it is our obedience to the prodding or nudging of the Spirit that opens up the floodgates to the anointing. For instance, there may be times when the Spirit is leading us in one direction, but because of our own fleshly desires, we choose the opposite direction. Where there is disobedience, there is a lack of anointing.

Remember: His will and purpose plus your obedience to

the Spirit equals the visible evidence of God's supernatural power—His great anointing, and a surplus of victories.

FINDING YOUR CALLING AND HIS ANOINTING

One of the first things I said to you in this pocket was, "You were called, you have purpose, and there is greatness living inside you." This is true! But, oftentimes as we try to find our place, we may see someone in a powerful position or successfully embarking on a particular venture, and it piques our interest—naturally, as we are curious beings. But, unfortunately it may pique our interest to the point where we believe that we too can hold that same position or embark on that exact venture. What we fail to realize is that we may not be anointed to do what that person has been called to do.

When we do what God has *not* anointed us to do, the journey is twice as challenging. We may end up going in circles, making the same mistakes over and over again. When we do what God has *not* anointed us to do, everything we do and every effort we make will be made in the flesh, and therefore bounded by the limitations of the flesh. Basically, there will be no "supernatural on our natural" when we are working in the flesh—we are simply using our limited knowledge and limited skills to open limited doors.

> GOD WILL NOT ONLY GIVE YOU DREAMS AND VISIONS BUT WILL ALSO SPEAK—HIS SPIRIT TO YOUR SPIRIT—NUDGING YOU TO DO SOMETHING, GO SOMEWHERE, OR SEE SOMETHING.

This is why it's imperative that we find God's specific will, purpose, and calling for our lives. As we embark on this journey, we must resist the temptation to walk in another person's anointing—we must be confident in knowing that our anointing is unique to us. We are called to do great things through our unique anointing—it is ours and no one else's.

Okay, so now that we've gotten that out the way, here are some of the ways to find your calling and God's anointing:

Commune with the Holy Spirit. Start by developing an intimate relationship with the Holy Spirit, acknowledging the Spirit of God that lives within you. Know that the Spirit teaches and leads if you allow Him to. You are never alone—the Holy Spirit is always with you. And although you may be accustomed to being self-reliant, you must begin to include the Spirit in every decision you make in your life. This is not the time to make your own decisions based on what you feel. No, this is the time to include the Helper, the one given to us through Christ Jesus, who is there to help us. When we acknowledge Him in all things, commune with the Spirit of God in all things, He helps us in all things. He is also the Spirit of Truth, "guiding us into all truth" (John 16:13). Therefore when we yield, He will always lead us on the right path, and this makes finding our calling, purpose, and God's will that much easier.

Trust the Spirit of God to lead you; develop a relationship with Him; lean on Him; seek and rely on Him for divine wisdom, knowledge, and understanding. Start thanking God for the Holy Spirit, and then begin to commune with the Spirit. Include the Spirit in the decisions you make on a daily basis. Ask God to show you His purpose and will for your life. Ask Him for direction, dreams and visions. Ask Him to show you your path, and He will through His Spirit. Remember: His will and purpose plus your obedience to the leadership of the Holy Spirit equals His anointing.

Fasting with Prayer. In addition to developing a relationship with the Holy Spirit, an effective way of finding your purpose and calling is through fasting with prayer. It is not a requirement, but fasting with prayer is highly recommended for this leg of the journey. Prayers should already be a part of your daily life, but when combined with fasting you have the Kingdom's full attention. Fasting draws us into deeper intimacy with God. It is the act of voluntarily giving up some or all physical food, habits and/or behaviors in exchange for spiritual nourishment and growth. Fasting with prayers is one of the means by which we hear from God and He moves on our behalf. It is not manipulating God into doing what we want Him to do. It is giving up our fleshly desires in order to be brought closer to Him. We seek Him with supplications and He honors our sacrifice by attending to our needs according to His will for our lives.

Note that unless it is a team or group effort—a fast with one's church or a friend—fasting is also *not* an act for all to see. In fact, in Matthew 6:16-18, Jesus instructs us by saying: "When you fast, do not be like the hypocrites, with a sad countenance. For they disfigure their faces that they may appear to men to be fasting. Assuredly, I say to you, they have their reward. But you, when you fast, anoint your head and wash your face, so that you do not appear to men to be fasting, but to your Father who is in the secret place; and your Father who sees in secret will reward you openly." Fasting is simply an act between you and God. It is an act of humility—casting aside food and worldly goods in exchange for His presence, His counsel, His direction.

There are no set rules for fasting. One person may fast for a day or two and another may embark on a thirty day fast—it is simply a matter of choice and obedience to the Spirit. There are also no set rules for the times of fasting. Many people fast from sunrise to sunset; others fast from 6 a.m. to 6 p.m. or from 7 a.m. to 1 p.m.—again, it's a matter of choice.

Now, let me just say at this: For all who may hope to lose weight—you know who you are!—please do not let that be your motivation to embark on a spiritual fast. I know, believe me, I know that you want desperately to fit into that dress or suit you bought months ago and still haven't worn yet. The one that you look at every day and think, "If I can just drop five more pounds it will fit." Trust me, I feel your pain. But, that is not what fasting is about. Fasting is a spiritual discipline and must be approached as such—it is *not* a quick-fix weight-loss program.

Fasting should also *not* become a "religious" ritual, with no basis, reason, or cause. All throughout the bible, people fasted for specific reasons. They fasted to honor God; to repent; to receive a revelation; to be delivered; to be healed; for revival and simply to humble themselves before God. Fasting must be for a specific purpose or purposes.

In this particular case, we may fast and pray for revelation about our specific calling, "that we might humble ourselves before our God, to seek from Him the right way for us" (Ezra8:21). It is through this process that we strip ourselves of worldly resources and focus our attention on our Father, taking to His throne our need for clarity and divine direction for this new journey.

Please Note: If you have never fasted before, <u>do not embark on a fast until you truly understand how to fast</u>. Seek advice from your church or purchase additional materials on spiritual fasting.

<u>Dreams and Visions.</u> Once you begin to pray for direction, get ready, because God will give you dreams and visions about where He desires to lead you. Visions are what we see in the mind's eye while awake; they are the images and/or scenes communicated through the Holy Spirit. Dreams are what we see in the mind's eye while asleep; they are also images and/or scenes communicated through the Holy Spirit. It is important that we pay attention to the dreams and visions God gives us. Make it

a habit to journal all your dreams and visions, including the emotions attached to them at the time of the experience and your revelations or thoughts on them. If you are not clear about the interpretation of the dream, ask God to make it clear to you. Ask Him for interpretation and revelation, and He will supply it through His Spirit. Eventually it will all be revealed to you.

<u>Pay Attention to the NOTHS.</u> As we continue to pray for His will and our calling, it is important to pay attention to what I call the NOTHS—"nudging of the Holy Spirit." God will not only give you dreams and visions but will also speak—His Spirit to your spirit—nudging you to do something, go somewhere, or see something. It is that feeling that you just can't shake, that churning in the pit of your stomach that's telling you to move or not to move. It is that thing that seems to pop up everywhere: you turn on the television and something relating to the nudge is on; you open a magazine and see something that reminds you about the nudge. Pay attention! That may well be God speaking to you about what you are called to do.

It may be that you are unemployed and during your job search you come across a position that you would love to apply to, but you think that you may be unqualified. So, you move on, but *something* keeps telling you to apply. You try to ignore it, but you go to bed still thinking about this particular position. Despite your efforts to put the thought behind you, you just keep thinking about this position. Well, this is a classic example of a NOTHS. What you are feeling is the nudging of the Spirit, poking you to do what God has already anointed you to do. It is at this point that your obedience to the Holy Spirit comes into play. This is when you must yield and obey. Now, you may be thinking, "Yeah, but I don't think I qualify." Well, I am here to tell you that God rarely calls the qualified but qualifies those He has called. You have favor, so yield.

Confirming the Call

So, now you're getting the dreams, some visions and experiencing some NOTHS. You think you know what God wants you to become, what He has anointed you to do, but you're not totally sure. This is the time to ask God for confirmation. It is important to get confirmation from God before you proceed, because the fact is that not every "great" idea is from God. Some ideas are nothing but the trick of the enemy to distract and delay us from the purpose for which God has called us.

> SO OFTEN WE MISS WHAT GOD IS SAYING BECAUSE WE FAIL TO RECOGNIZE WHEN HE IS TALKING TO US.

Getting God's confirmation on everything that I do is now such a huge part of my life. I have gotten to the place where I do not want to make a move unless God tells me to. I want what God wants for me and only what He wants. God knows all His children, and He knows that I am the person who will see one thing and analyze it a million different ways. So whenever I seek confirmation, I often remind my Father to make it so clear that there can be no misinterpretations.

You must adopt a level of transparency when you commune with God—remember that you are one of His children. Ask Him to confirm that this direction is His will for your life. Express a desire for His will and pray that He removes all doubt and confusion, knowing that "He is not the author of confusion but of peace" (1 Corinthians 14:33). Once you've made your request known to the Father through prayer, keep your eyes open and pay attention. If it is His will, God will confirm it, and the Holy Spirit will testify to its truth with His indescribable peace.

Oftentimes when God confirms He confirms in threes. Why? Because the number three is the biblical number of completion—as in the Godhead, "Father, Son, and Holy Ghost." All throughout the bible the number three signifies divine completion or fulfillment. "Jonah was in the belly of the fish for *three* days and *three* nights" (Jonah 1:17) before it spat him out; Jesus was buried for *three* days before He was raised from the dead; *three* wise men brought baby Jesus gold, frankincense, and myrrh; Peter denied Christ *three* times; we are told to "abide in faith, hope and love" (1 Corinthians 13:13); we are *trifold* beings made up of body, mind, spirit; heavenly creatures cry out, "Holy, Holy, Holy" (Revelation 4:8). Even in our society today, we have subconsciously acknowledged the significance of the trifold with popular phrases like "the third time is the charm," "three cheers," and "three wishes." Therefore, if God confirms three times, take that as a green light and go for it!

Keep in mind that when God confirms, He may do so by any means or medium. So again, pay attention! So often we miss what God is saying because we fail to recognize when He is talking to us. We are so caught up in our thoughts that we fail to see the subtle signs and signals He gives us. God speaks, but we must be alert. We must still our minds and quiet our thoughts long enough to hear Him.

> GOD HAS ALREADY LAID OUT A PATH OF SUCCESS FOR YOU. HE HAS ALREADY PUT THE DIVINE CONNECTIONS IN PLACE. HE HAS ALREADY ANOINTED YOU TO ACCOMPLISH EVERYTHING HE HAS CALLED YOU TO DO.

The first place God may confirm our calling, His will and purpose is in His Word. This is why meditating on the Word of God, as opposed to simply reading it, is important—meditation brings forth revelation. God will give us confirmation through His word. It may be during your daily devotional, or it may be a sermon preached at church, or through a television ministry. Despite the where or how, His Word will always be "a lamp to your feet and a light to your *path*" (Psalm 119:105).

Confirmation may also come through another individual. You may randomly run into a friend, who says, "Hey, I think you should do XYZ. I think you would be good at it." It may be a prophetic word spoken to you which confirms what God has already been revealing to you. It may also come through the media. You may open the newspaper or magazine and find an article relating to where you believe God is leading you. It may be a television program that sparks your interest. It may be anything or through anyone, but regardless, it means that God is confirming what He has already spoken into your spirit. Keep your ears and eyes open. Be alert—but not anxious.

It is important to note that confirmation may not come immediately. If that is the case, make an effort not to be anxious, but instead to surrender to the process. Surrendering does not mean that you're giving up, but it means that you trust God enough to lead you and guide you on the right path. Rest in the belief that as His child, you are anointed and that He has great things in store for you. It is as simple as that: You are His child and He is obligated to lead you on the right path—if you have faith.

As your heavenly Father, God has already laid out a path of success for you. He has already put the divine connections in place. He has already anointed you to accomplish everything He has called you to do. Surrendering means saying, "Lord, I know you love me and you have great things in store for me. I look to you expectantly for direction and for confirmation. I thank you that everything and everyone is already in place to accomplish all that you are calling me to do." And then you rest. Trust and believe that if

> WHEN THE ANOINTING OF GOD IS UPON YOU TO DO SOMETHING, YOU ARE GUARANTEED SUCCESS AND EFFORTLESS VICTORIES.

it's God's will for your life, He will confirm it. If there is no confirmation then it's simply not His will.

Continue to ask, look, and listen. Think of the Holy Spirit as your personal spiritual navigational system, leading you: "Turn right; then two miles ahead, make a sharp turn left; you've arrived at your destination on your right." We know that when we follow the NOTHS, when we pay attention to our dreams and visions, when we seek Him first, we are guaranteed to be led on the divine pathway to a victoriously fulfilling life.

ANOINTED, CALLED, AND READY TO GO

So at this point you are sure—you know without a doubt what God has called you to do. You have received all the confirmation you needed. Now what? Now you go and do it! Go for it! There is nothing you cannot do when the power of God is working through you.

What He has anointed you to do may seem outside of your comfort zone; you may not be familiar with the industry; you may not have the technical expertise required to succeed naturally; you may feel overwhelmed; you may feel out of place and inferior to others in the field. But, please note that when the anointing of God is upon you to do something, you are guaranteed success and effortless victories.

1 Corinthians 1:27 (NLT) reminds us that "God chose things the world considers foolish in order to shame those who think they are wise and he chose things that are power-

less to shame those who are powerful." You are the one God has chosen. Not your friend, not your family member, not your spouse, not your coworker—you!

The enemy may start bombarding your mind with negative thoughts like: "You can't do that," "Who do you think you are? You are nobody, so just quit," "You're just being silly: no one in your family has ever been that successful and you won't be either," "No one is going to take you seriously, so you might as well give up now," or "You know you are not smart enough to do that." The lies will go on and on, if you allow them. Resist, renounce, rebuke, renew, and speak life!

> THE ANOINTING OF GOD BREAKS YOKES, DESTROYS BARRIERS, AND CREATES PATHS WHERE NONE PREVIOUSLY EXISTED.

You may even find yourself being challenged, laughed at, and ridiculed by some of the people you thought for sure would support you. Initially there may be naysayers and backbiters at every turn, but that's all a part of the work of the enemy. The enemy's goal is to dissuade you, discourage you, play on your insecurities, play on your fears, remind you of your past failures, remind you of your shortcomings, remind you of your economic conditions, remind you of your family history, remind you of every "bad" and "shameful" thing you may have done. His plan is to get you outside of the will of God, to destroy your hopes and dreams and prevent you from living a joyfully fulfilling life. Rebuke these negative thoughts, dismiss the cynics, and diligently pursue the purposes of God.

Keep in mind that you are a new being in Christ—your past is your past. You are forgiven and now you are anointed to do great things in the name of Jesus. It does not matter how big the task seems or how impossible it seems for you, the anointing of God breaks yokes, destroys barriers, and creates paths where none previously existed.

As you step out in faith, know that God will unravel His plans for your success. As you surrender to His will and trust in His power, He will reveal each step of His plans through the dreams, visions, and NOTHS. Surrendering and trusting at this point is critical. Sometimes we are so excited about what the visions and dreams represent that if we are not careful, we begin to rely on our efforts instead of on God. We sometimes subconsciously step ahead of God—we receive the vision with great enthusiasm and immediately run off with our own ideas before God has the chance to speak to us about His path. Surrendering and trusting allows God to take the lead, while we follow.

Once we grasp that this is His work through us, and not our doing, we are then able to rest and let Him lead and direct us. This is when suddenly you are at the right place at the right time to make the right connections. This is when He will give you a revelation for each level of the journey and what may have initially seemed confusing will become crystal clear. The path that originally seemed crooked will suddenly become straight, and what you could not have done before, you are suddenly able to do with minimal effort. That, my friends, is the anointing, the fresh oil of God.

There is nothing on the face of the earth that you cannot do when God has anointed you to do it. Be steadfast and move forward with the vision. Develop what I call a "tunnel-vision drive"—an ambitious drive that will not permit you to look to your left nor right, but requires you to look straight ahead toward the goal, focusing on what God has called you to do.

> ANOINTING BLOCKERS ARE SPIRITUAL LEVEES THAT HINDER THE FLOW OF THE POWER OF GOD IN OUR LIVES.

When God has called and anointed you to do something, do it! You are anointed; you have the fresh oil of God upon you; you have His divine power working in you. Therefore you "can do all things through Christ who strengthens you" (Philippians 4:13). The anointing guarantees victories. All you have to do is stay attached to the "true vine—Jesus Christ" (John 15:1), and you will be fruitful and victorious in all that you do.

Continuous Flow

As we embark on this journey—living, working, and walking in this great anointing—it is important that we stay clear of anointing blockers. Anointing blockers are spiritual levees that hinder the flow of the power of God in our lives. It is anything that blocks us from the anointing power of the Holy Spirit. It prevents us from effectively functioning in the Kingdom to accomplish its purposes, from doing successfully what we have been called to do.

There are several things that may be categorized as anointing blockers. These may include but are not limited to: strife, unforgivingness, disobedience, anger, resentment, constant murmuring, envy, fear, hatred and so much more. We must remember that in everything we do, as believers, we must have faith and gratitude, and our foundation must be based on love—the love of God and love for one another. When we walk in obedience to the commandment to love, God's glory will be revealed in everything that we do, and He will be faithful to bless all the work of our hands (Deuteronomy 28:8).

> DO AND BE ALL GOD HAS CALLED YOU TO BE! YOU ARE CALLED TO DO AND ACCOMPLISH AMAZING THINGS.

Jesus said, "Without Me, you can do nothing" (John 15:5), and that's exactly it. Without the anointing of God we cannot accomplish anything that makes a lasting, significant impact on the world and on the Kingdom of God. Therefore, if for some reason it seems that your anointing is not flowing as it should—that there is a block—stop to see if you've built up a spiritual levee somewhere along the journey. When you've pinpointed the block, demolish it with a prayer for forgiveness, a repented heart, and a determination to release it from your life.

EMBRACE YOUR GREATNESS

Having the full knowledge about what you have been called to do and being sure that you are where God wants you to be is one of the most spiritually, emotionally, mentally, physically, and oftentimes financially rewarding things you could ever experience. In your quest, know that the road may not be completely free of humps and bumps, but I encourage you to never give up, and always seek God first for His will and purpose in every area of your life. In doing so, your path will be made clear, your joy bountiful, and you will have endless victories through the power of the anointing.

Do and be all God has called you to be! You are called to do and accomplish amazing things. There is purpose for your life and there is power and greatness living inside of you. Press on and see the victories in Jesus's name!

MAKE YOUR OWN NOTES

What do you believe God has anointed you to do?

_____
_____
_____
_____
_____
_____
_____
_____

> "THE HELPER, THE HOLY SPIRIT, WHOM THE FATHER WILL SEND IN MY NAME, HE WILL TEACH YOU ALL THINGS."
>
> ~ JOHN 14:26

_____
_____
_____
_____
_____
_____
_____
_____
_____
_____
_____
_____
_____
_____

POCKET 8

ARSENAL OF VICTORIES

I cannot carry a tune to save my life, but when I'm in church I sing and praise the loudest. In fact, standing at a distance, you may think that I'm a natural-born singer—I look confident in my singing abilities and I sing my heart out. I praise, worship, and sing, sing, sing. Now, if you were standing to my left and to my right—well, let's just say that there would be no mistaking it. You would immediately know that I am somewhat tone-deaf, singing out of tune and definitely off pitch. But, do I care? No! Why not? Because I was born to sing my God praises.

> IT IS THROUGH PRAYER, GRATITUDE, AND PRAISE THAT DELIVERANCE TAKES PLACE, MIRACLES OCCUR, AND LIVES ARE CHANGED FOREVER.

God has been so good to me. The thought of His goodness overwhelms me. He snatched me out of this world, washed me in His blood, sanctified me, set me free, and I am so grateful. I can see now that in all that I've been through, He was always there. He was there and has always been there just waiting for me to surrender, just waiting for me let go of all that I thought the world had to offer. He was there.

He was there when my earthly father rejected me; He was there when my "prince" broke my heart. He was there in the restaurant; He was there in the midst of the trials and tribulations. He was there in the midst of business failures. He was there in the hospital. He was there when I was lost and couldn't find my way. He was there through it all—arms wide open, waiting with His indescribable peace, unspeakable joy, and unfathomable love, waiting for me to concede.

He is an awesome God, filled with love and mercy. He is a "Mighty Savior" (Isaiah 19:20), a "Wonderful Counselor, Mighty God, Everlasting Father, Prince of Peace" (Isaiah 9:6). He is my "Redeemer" (Isaiah 47:4), the "King of Kings and Lord of Lords" (Revelation 19:16), the "Alpha and the Omega, the Beginning and the End, the First and the Last" (Revelations 22:13). There's no one like Him. There's no greater name than the name of Jesus! I glorify and magnify His Holy name. Today, my soul cries Holy, Holy, Holy—Lord you are Holy!

THE MIGHTY TRIAD

Pray, give thanks, and praise God in all things and at all times. Prayer, gratitude, and praise are three major components to living victoriously. Individually they are the means by which we communicate and commune with God; collectively they serve as the weapons of spiritual warfare, tearing down strongholds, destroying barriers, and leading us into victory.

Prayer, gratitude, and praise are a mighty triad and should not be a "Sunday-only event." In order to truly live victoriously, it must be a daily, lifelong event. Praying, giving thanks, shouting for joy, and praising God on Sunday or Saturday, (depending on your denomination), but neglecting to spend time in prayer, neglecting to thank and praise Him Monday through Saturday, makes us nothing but "religious."

We are not called to be "religious" but we are called to "worship God in spirit and in truth" (John 4:24). We are called into an intimate relationship with Him, through His Word and with prayer, gratitude, and praise.

The act of praying, giving thanks, and praising should be born from our deep, sincere, abiding love for God. A love that wants more of Him, more of His presence, more of His glory, more, more, more—more of who He is. It should not be considered a burdensome obligation. It should be fueled by our love and motivated by our desires to please Him.

> PRAYERS ARE A LIFELINE TO THE BELIEVER. THEY ARE THE SPIRITUAL VENTILATORS THAT KEEP US LIVING, MOVING, AND HAVING OUR BEING IN GOD.

It is through prayer, gratitude, and praise that the essence of God is revealed. It is through prayer, gratitude, and praise that our enemies are defeated and victories won. It is through prayer, gratitude, and praise that deliverance takes place, miracles occur, and lives are changed forever. Pray, give thanks, and praise God in all things and at all times!

Prayer

Prayer is the means by which we speak to God. It is our spiritually dedicated communication line between us and Abba, Father. It is the means by which we dial into the heavenly connection—corresponding with God, acknowledging who He is and entering into His Most Holy Place.

It is imperative that, as believers, we develop and maintain an active prayer life. When facing trials, our first action should always be to pray. Our second should always be to get into the Word of God, finding scriptures relating to our particular situations, for "men always ought to pray and not lose heart" (Luke 18:1).

Unfortunately, oftentimes prayer is a second thought—sometimes a third, fourth, or fifth thought in times of trials. We are inclined to worry, murmur, wail, cry, get angry, and get on the phone with everyone, while prayer is an afterthought. Instead of worrying and complaining, we must develop the habit of giving it all to God in prayer—leaving it at the altar, leaving it at His throne, leaving it at His feet. God is faithful to hear us, deliver us, and strengthen us in the battle. The reality is that, at the end of the day, no one can help or provide like God can—no one. Give it all to Him in prayer.

Prayers are a lifeline to the believer. They are the spiritual ventilators that keep us living, moving, and having our being in God. It is through prayer that we "enter into His gates with thanksgiving and His courts with praise" (Psalm 100:4). It is through prayer that we are able draw upon His strength to take us through the valleys of our lives. It is through prayer that we "make our requests be known to God" (Philippians 4:6). It is through prayer that we intercede on behalf of others, entering into spiritual warfare, binding the works of the enemy, and loosening the covering of God. It is through prayer, through daily communication with God, that we live victoriously.

We must develop and maintain an active prayer life, much like Jesus did. Even Christ, the Son of God, made prayer a part of His daily life. It was through the act of praying that Jesus, during His earthly ministry, kept in constant communication with the Father. All throughout the Gospel, Jesus called upon and drew strength from God through prayer. "While He prayed, the heaven was opened and the Holy Spirit descended in bodily form like a dove upon Him" (Luke 3:21) and "as He prayed" His appearance changed and He was transfigured on the mountain (Luke 9:29). It was when "He went a little farther and fell on His face, and prayed" (Matthew 26:39) that He drew strength from the Father for what was to come at the cross. Jesus's prayer life was continuous: "He went out to the mountain to pray, and continued all night in prayer to God" (Luke 6:12); it was planned: "He was praying in a certain place" (Luke 11:1); and it was private: "Now in the morning, having risen a long while before daylight, He went out and departed to a solitary place; and there He prayed" (Mark 1:35). Jesus, the Son of the Living God, prayed often, and in order to live victoriously we too must follow suit and "pray without ceasing" (1 Thessalonians 5:17).

> TAKE TIME FIRST THING IN THE MORNING TO ENTER INTO THE PRESENCE OF GOD THROUGH PRAYER. THIS IS AN ACT OF GIVING GOD YOUR FIRST FRUITS.

Pray Without Ceasing

It took me a while to truly understand what "pray without ceasing" meant. I thought, "How does one pray without ceasing?" Like many people, I thought there was a particular way to pray: get down on one's knees, close one's eyes, and commence to pray. "How could I possibly do that without ceasing? Can anyone pray without ceasing?" I wondered. Well, I now know that yes, we can pray without ceasing, and we must. I've learned that, while it is imperative that we humble ourselves before God, honor Him, and show reverence by kneeling in prayer, praying is not limited to these actions.

When we pray without ceasing, we are simply communing with God throughout the day. A simple "Lord, I love you and thank you for this day" as you take a stroll is an act of prayer. A simple "Lord, I just acknowledge your presence with me always" as you are sitting at your desk is an act of prayer. All communication between you and God is an act of prayer. It may be a silent prayer, a whispered prayer, or an audible prayer, but regardless, as believers we must pray without ceasing.

Pray in your car. Pray on your job. Pray while taking a walk. Pray while working out at the gym. Pray in your school. Pray in the doctor's office. Pray in the hallway. Pray in your home. Pray as you travel. Pray in the grocery store. Pray, pray, pray—never cease to pray.

As you develop your prayer life, if at all possible, take time first thing in the morning to enter into the presence of

God through prayer. This is an act of giving God your first fruits: the first of your day and the best of your day. Psalm 63:1 says, "Early will I seek you." Giving God the first of yourself in the morning is essentially an act of declaration—declaring that He is the center and strength of your life. It is also the means by which we are spiritually strengthened for the day ahead.

As you maintain your prayer life, you'll discover that on the days that you are just a bit too busy to pray, on the mornings that you rush out of your home to make it to work on time, on the mornings that you scramble to get everyone together and out the door, on the days you have back-to-back meetings, on the days with a full school or work schedule, your spirit will yearn for a spirit-to-Spirit dialogue with God. You may discover that at the end of that busy day, there is a feeling of emptiness, a feeling that something is missing. There may be a stirring in your spirit to just get down on your knees and enter into His presence. This is because throughout the day, your spirit craved that heavenly connection through prayer and now it is in need of rejuvenation—surrender to the spirit and pray.

> PRAYERS ARE NOT REHEARSED LINES, AND TECHNICALLY THERE IS NO WRONG WAY OR RIGHT WAY TO PRAY.

"In His presence is fullness of joy" (Psalm 16:11), and as we pray without ceasing, we will soon discover that in the middle of the most challenging times, we are filled with joy. When people around us are losing their minds from stress, we are "kept in perfect peace because our minds stay on God" (Isaiah 26:3). As we choose to "set our minds on the things above and not the things on the earth" (Colossians 3:2), as we continue to put God first, He will be faithful to direct our paths. Everything that we are seeking, all the victories we desire "will be added unto us" (Matthew 6:33), according to our faith and His will.

Effective Prayers

I've heard people say over and over again, "I don't know how to pray" or "I'm not sure that God hears my prayers—maybe I'm not praying the right way." The thunder-rolling, passionate prayers of others sometimes intimidate us, leaving us feeling that our prayers are inadequate and ineffective. Every so often, we even go so far as to compare the length of time spent in prayer with others: "I don't get it. Steven spent three hours this morning in prayer and I only spent ten minutes. What's wrong with me?" But there is nothing wrong with you; your ten minutes spent in prayer may be much more effective than Steven's three hours spent in prayer.

For some reason, many believers think that we all have to look, talk, walk, and act the same, even as it relates to praying. But prayers are not rehearsed lines, and technically there is no wrong way or right way to pray. What we must do is allow ourselves to be led by the Holy Spirit in prayer. In doing so, we avoid placing human expectations on the time, length, and type of prayer that we make.

When led by the Spirit, our prayers may be as short as the Sprit leads, or as long as the Spirit leads; as passionate or as compassionate, as the Spirit leads; in heavenly tongues or our native tongue, as the Spirit leads. There are no preconceived notions and no human limitations, when the Spirit leads.

I must admit that for many years, I truly did not understand certain aspects of praying, like the significance of kneeling or the importance of praying in Jesus' name. These two particular aspects were a bit of a mystery to me, and they remained a mystery until I began renewing my mind with the Word of God. It was then I understood who I was, whose I was, why we kneel, and why the name of Jesus is so important in prayer.

> IT IS OUR PRAYERS IN FAITH—OUR BELIEF THAT GOD HEARS US AND THAT HE IS FAITHFUL—THAT ALLOWS THE REQUESTS MADE IN PRAYER TO BECOME VISIBLE MANIFESTATIONS IN OUR LIVES.

Today, from the depths of my heart, I kneel to pray—not because everyone else is doing it, but because God loves me so much and that love fills my heart. I humbly kneel before my Lord in reverence, honoring Him and glorifying His name. Today, I now know that while "technically" there are no right or wrong ways in which to pray, there are keys to an effective prayer:

- *Pray in faith:* When we pray, we must believe that because we are His children, God hears our prayers.

Know by faith, by virtue of your relationship to Him through Christ, that your prayers are heard. By faith, "we know he hears us when we make our requests, we also know that he will give us what we ask for" (1 John 5:15 NLT). Pray in faith, believing that everything He says you are, everything He says you have, and everything He has promised in His word is true and available to you. It is our prayers in faith—our belief that God hears us and that He is faithful—that allows the requests made in prayer to become visible manifestations in our lives.

- *Pray in righteousness:* Righteousness means "right standing with God" or "proper relationship between man and God." We know that no man is truly sinless, but we also know that through faith in Jesus Christ we are reconciled and "God imputes righteousness" (Romans 4:6) in us through His Spirit. As a result, our lives should bear the fruit of God's righteousness working in us. Therefore, Mark 11:25 instructs us, "Whenever you stand praying, if you have anything against anyone, forgive him, that your Father in heaven may also forgive you your trespasses," and Matthew 5:23-24 says, "Therefore if you bring your gift to the altar, and there remember that your brother has something against you, leave your gift there before the altar, and go your way. First be reconciled to your brother, and then come and offer your gift." God is a righteous God and desires for us, His children, to walk upright. When we are sure to forgive, to not hold on to grudges, to not harbor deceit and hatred, to not hold anything against our fellow man, and to repent with our hearts, we can be sure that He hears us. According to Proverbs 15:29: "The lord is far from the wicked, but He hears the prayer of the righteous." When we pray in righteousness, we are assured that "the effective, fervent prayer of a righteous man avails much" (James 5:16).

- *Pray in the matchless and mighty name of Jesus*: It took me a while to understand the significance of praying in the name of Jesus. It was not until I began seeking God and truly reading and understanding the scriptures that the significance was revealed to me. It was in reading about my Lord and Savior Jesus Christ—understanding who He is to me, what He did for me, who I am, and why I have access to the blessings—that my prayers became truly effective. My "wow moment" was when I read John 16:23-24, where Jesus says: "Most assuredly, I say to you, whatever you ask the Father in *My name* He will give you. Until now you have asked nothing in *My name*. Ask, and *you will receive*, that your joy may be full." Remember: The only reason that we are heirs to the Abrahamic covenant, and that the promises of God are available to us is because of the death and resurrection of Jesus Christ. Jesus has all power and authority in heaven and in the earth. It is "through faith in our Lord we have boldness and access" (Ephesians 3:11-12) to enter the presence of God and make our requests known before

His throne. Therefore, we can be confident that when we pray in the name of Jesus, "if we ask anything in His name, He will do it" (John 14:14), according to His divine purpose and will for our lives.

- *Pray according to His will:* Praying according to His will is praying according to the Word of God, and His word "shall not return to Him void, But it shall accomplish what He pleases, and it shall prosper in the thing for which He sent it." Oftentimes we pray, beg, and beg some more but always fail to speak His Word in prayer. Remember the Word of God is His promises to us, and as His children we must remind our Father of His promises. In Pocket 6, I described some of the characteristics of a child and mentioned that if you make a promise to a child, every time you see the child, he or she will always remind you of the promise: "Remember you said you were going to take me to the zoo!" Well, that's what we, as children of God, need to do in prayer—speak His Word and repeat His promises in prayer: "Lord, remember according to your Word, all things work together for my good because I love and I'm called according to your purpose," or "Lord, I look to you for the exceedingly abundantly, above all I ask or think according to your Word," or "Lord, I receive your peace because your Word says that you leave your peace with me. You've given me peace, not as the world gives peace; your peace surpasses all understanding." "This is the confidence that we have in Him, that if we ask anything according to His will, He hears us" (1 John 5:14). Effective prayers are those that incorporate the Word of God—those prayed according to His will.

- *Pray like it's already done:* Start thanking God for everything you've asked for in Jesus' name and according to His will. Now, you may think, "How do I thank Him if I don't have it yet?" Again, remember: Faith is not hoping in that which is seen but in that which is not yet seen. Believe by faith that everything you are seeking God for has already been done and start thanking Him. "Lord, I thank you that according to your Word, no weapons formed against me shall prosper." "Lord, I thank you that I am more than a conquering. I have a surpassing victory in Christ Jesus, according to your Word." "Lord, I thank you that I lack nothing, need nothing, because you supply all my needs according to Your riches in glory by Christ Jesus." "Lord, I thank you that by your stripes, by your blood, and according to your Word, I am healed." Think about this: If you ask someone to bring you a cup of tea, you will not usually wait for the person to physically bring the tea before you thank him or her. Typically, you ask and thank the individual in advance, all in the same breath: "Hey, Sam, can you please bring me back a cup of tea? Thanks!" Well, in the same way that we thank each other in advance, we must thank God in advance for all that we've asked of Him in prayer. "Continue earnestly in prayer, being vigilant in it *with* thanksgiving" (Colossians 4:2) and "in everything by prayer and supplication, *with* thanksgiving, let your requests be made known to God" (Philippians 4:6). Thanking God in advance is the way by which we exercise our faith in prayer. We are thanking God, believing, having faith in His Word that tells us "whatever things you ask when you pray, believe that you receive them, and you will have them" (Mark 11:24). If you truly believe that what you've asked for you'll have—if you know that you have prayed in the name of Jesus, that you are in right standing with God, that you have asked according to His will, then stop asking God for the same things over and over again. He heard you the first time! Effectively exercise your faith by thanking Him, believing that "His will be done on earth as it is in heaven" (Luke 2:2), believing that what you've asked for has already been done in the heavenly realm, and believing that you will receive the manifestations in the earthly realm. Start thanking God today.

INTERCESSORY PRAYERS

As we "continue steadfastly in prayer" (Romans 12:12), it is important that we pay attention to our thoughts and the images in our mind's eyes during prayer. In the course of praying, God may give us images, visions, and/or speak into our spirits about a partic-

> IT IS THROUGH PRAYERS, DREAMS, AND VISIONS THAT GOD REVEALS THE PLANS OF THE ENEMY IN THE SPIRITUAL REALM.

ular person or situation. It may simply be the name of a particular person that keeps coming into our thoughts, or it may be the quick flash of a person's face in our mind's eye, or it may be full visions of people, places, and situations. Whatever they are, do not ignore them, as this is the work of the Holy Spirit calling us into intercessory prayer.

Intercessory prayer is the means by which we intercede on behalf of another through prayer. It is the means by which we stand in the gap, filling in the crack in the faith of another. It is a spiritual intervention, the act of intervening through prayerful petitions on behalf of another.

We are called to be "good soldiers of Jesus Christ" (2 Timothy 2:3), and as soldiers, we may be called into battle from time to time. Now we know that "for though we walk (live) in the flesh, we are not carrying on our warfare according to the flesh and using mere human weapons. For the weapons of our warfare are not physical—weapons of flesh and blood—but they are mighty before God for the overthrow and destruction of strongholds" (2 Corinthians 10:3-4 AMP).

It is through prayers, dreams, and visions that God reveals the plans of the enemy in the spiritual realm. He shows us the traps and the plots to kill, steal, and destroy our lives and the lives of others. It is for us, soldiers in the army of God, to enter into spiritual battle, binding up the works of the enemy, casting down the plots and plans of the enemy, and bringing to naught every weapon that tries to form against us and others in the name of Jesus. It is for us to put on the "whole armor of God" (Ephesians 6:11), which empowers us to win on behalf of another. It is for us to "labor fervently for others in prayers" (Colossians 4:12), "praying always in the Spirit—at all times interceding on behalf of others" (Ephesian 6:18).

We must be mindful of the work of the Holy Spirit during sessions of prayer. We must be careful not to "quench the Spirit" (1 Thessalonian 5:19) by resisting His work through us. Intercessory prayers are powerful tools to victory, used for the benefit of another. It is through intercessory prayers that we, servants of God, have the power and authority through Jesus Christ to intervene, thus preventing the destruction of another. It is through intercessory prayers that we may be led to petition for mercy from God for another, healing for another, deliverance for another, breakthroughs for another, protection for another, salvation for another—overall victory for another.

> IT IS OUR FAITH-FILLED EXPECTANCY THAT HAS US THANKING GOD IN ADVANCE, OPENING THE EVER-REVOLVING DOORS OF VICTORY.

Pray

Pray in faith always. Offer supplications to God, make your request known through prayer, pray for another, and intercede on behalf of another. Come into agreement, having one mind in prayer and having faith that "if two of you agree on earth concerning anything that they ask, it will be done for them by My Father in heaven" (Matthew 18:19). Our faithful prayers to God will not go unheard—He hears us, we are

His children, and He knows us by our names. By faith, believe that your petitions have already been fulfilled, that you already have the victory through Jesus Christ.

HEART OF GRATITUDE

So, we know that thanking God in advance is a powerful weapon that leads us into victory in all areas of our lives. I can't stress enough the importance of being mindful to thank God in advance for all you've asked of Him. It may seem a little awkward at first—forced, even—because after all, we live in a society that requires tangible evidence before gratitude. But, as citizens of the Kingdom of God, living according to His Word, we know that we already have the victory, and we boldly proclaim: "Thanks be to God, who gives us the victory through our Lord Jesus Christ!" (1 Corinthians 15:57).

> DO NOT BECOME DESENSITIZED TO THE GOODNESS OF GOD, BUT INSTEAD MAINTAIN A HEART OF GRATITUDE.

It is our faith-filled expectancy that has us thanking God in advance, opening the ever-revolving doors of victory. It is our knowledge of who we are—our royal identities as children of God—the knowledge of our heavenly Father and His faithful character that keeps us thanking God in advance. It is knowing and understanding the price paid by the blood of Jesus; knowing what His promises are to us, that keeps us thanking God in advance and receiving the victory.

At this point along the journey, you may be seeing the manifestations of the victories in your life. You've prayed and been faithful to God, and He has been exceedingly faithful to you. Now what? "I want to thank you all. Also, I want to thank my mom, my dad, my family, my best friend Stacy, my other best friend Kelly, my neighbor Steve, my cat Snooks, and my dog Ruff—without them, I would not have been able to do this. Thanks!" Is God anywhere in this picture? No, we must avoid this at all cost! It is important that as doors are opened, as opportunities are presented to us, and as we experience an increase in blessings, we do not become desensitized to the goodness of God, but instead maintain a heart of gratitude.

Whether you are a parent or not, imagine for a moment having a child and doing everything for that child. You cater to him, you give him whatever his heart desires, you comfort him when he is hurting, you bandage his wounds, you feed him, clothe him, protect him, you give him the best of everything and provide for his every need. You do all this, but you never or rarely receive a "thanks." Despite all that you do, this child seems to only want more, and there is simply no gratitude. When you—out of love for him and out of having his best interests at heart—deny him a request, you are confronted with an angry child who has an ungrateful heart. Imagine how painful that situation would be for you as a loving parent—you give, give, and give and receive no genuine appreciation in return. Now, if you can imagine that, then think of how God must feel when we fail to acknowledge His goodness and when we fail to give Him thanks. God is our heavenly Father, and He has done, is doing, and will do so much for us, but we must have hearts of gratitude and lips that utter thanksgiving.

There are so many things to be appreciative for on a daily basis. But it never ceases to amaze me how so many of us today are quick to thank so many things—people, animals, the universe—before we give thanks to God. Thanksgiving must first and always start with the giver of "every good and perfect gift" (James 1:16), the Holy Father.

In this life, and during these times, it is so easy for us to take the little things for granted. We see the blessings, we know we are blessed, but our hearts are not filled with gratitude—we simply want more and more. God has blessed us with so much. Initially we may give Him thanks, but as life takes form—as we experience the rollercoaster events of life—if we are not mindful, we may eventually find that our wells of gratitude to God have dried up. But, God is and has always been faithful to us despite our circumstances.

> GRATITUDE BRINGS TO LIGHT THE TRUE FAITH OF OUR HEARTS. A HEART THAT HAS LITTLE OR NO FAITH OFFERS LITTLE OR NO THANKSGIVING.

There are so many things we all need to be grateful to God for. So many blessings, seen and unseen: roof over our heads, clothes on our backs, shoes on our feet, food to eat, electricity, clean running water, the comforts of home, family, friends, functioning bodies, sound minds. "Oh, taste and see that the Lord is good!" (Psalm 34:8).

Have and maintain a heart of gratitude for past blessings, current blessings, and future blessings. Have and maintain a heart of gratitude for small blessings and large blessings. When we acknowledge the good works of our Father in every area of our lives, our gratitude will increase, and we'll experience the love of God in ways that we could never have imagined before. Each day, awake and "enter into His gates with thanksgiving, and into His courts with praise. Be thankful to Him, and bless His name. For the Lord is good; His mercy is everlasting" (Psalm 100:4-5).

When we have hearts of gratitude, we have hearts of joy. When we have hearts of gratitude, we are choosing to focus on the beauty of life and the goodness of God. Gratitude shifts our focus from lack to abundance. Gratitude brings to light the true faith of our hearts. A heart that has little or no faith offers little or no thanksgiving. But, a heart filled with faith offers thanksgiving to God at all times and in all things, in the valley and on the mountain top.

As I look at my life there are so, so, many things to thank God for. My heart is filled with gratitude for all God has done for me, in me, and through me. I give "thanks to God for His indescribable gift" (2 Corinthians 9:15), my Lord and Savior Jesus Christ. I've learned to have a heart of gratitude at all times, despite my circumstances. Every morning presents me with an opportunity to experience God's loving goodness in many different ways. I'm filled with gratitude when I'm able to look at the sky and see its beauty. I'm filled with gratitude when I'm able to hear the patter of raindrops against my window. I'm filled with gratitude when I'm able to feel the cool gush of wind against my skin on a hot summer day. I'm filled with gratitude when I'm in the comfort of a warm home while there is a winter storm brewing outside. I'm filled to the brim, overflowing with gratitude in all things because God is good!

> HAVING AND MAINTAIN A HEART OF GRATITUDE MOVES GOD, YIELDS UNSPEAKABLE JOY, AND COMMANDS THE VICTORIES.

I've experienced firsthand the victories that come with thanksgiving. I've learned and am still learning that instead of complaining about what I don't have or murmuring about what I do have, it is much healthier spiritually, mentally, and physically to trust God and be "content in whatever state I am" (Philippians 4:11). God is good and I am forever thankful and filled with gratitude.

"In everything give thanks, for this is the will of God in Christ Jesus for you" (1 Thessalonians 5:18). Have a heart of gratitude at all times, simply because God is good. Having and maintaining a heart of gratitude moves God, yields unspeakable joy, and commands the victories.

Praise Him!

I recently watched a video about a young twenty-two year old woman who had just been diagnosed with Multiple Sclerosis. Her message to the world was, "No matter your circumstances, praise God anyway." I then watched a follow-up video about her, and in it, all she did was sing praises to God. I could feel her deep, sincere love for God in every lyric; with tears running down her cheeks, she praised Him with all her heart. After drying my own tears, I stopped to think, "How many of us would have the faith to praise God in spite of such seemingly dismal circumstances?" Whether you were twenty-two or eighty-two, would you still have praise in your heart and on your lips in the midst of it all?

Praise is one of the most powerful means by which we receive victory. It was when Jehoshaphat appointed "those who should sing to the Lord, and who should praise the beauty of holiness and as they went out before the army and were saying: Praise the Lord, for His mercy endures forever" (2 Chronicles 20:21) that the "Lord set ambushes against" (2 Chronicles 20:22) their enemies, defeating them and giving Judah (which also means "praise") a surpassing victory.

There is mighty power in our praise, power that defeats our enemies, power that heals, power that delivers, power that restores, power that tears down barriers, power that breaks every stronghold and yoke—there is power in our praise to live victoriously.

PRAISING THROUGH IT

The power in our praise is activated by our faith in God, and although we know that there is power in our praise, oftentimes we find it difficult to praise God in the middle of our battles—we lament and we murmur, but we don't often praise. It is always easy to praise God when all is going well—when the children are finally behaving, when we are able to pay our bills, when the spouse is truly making an attempt to rekindle the fire, when the job is working out, when life itself is working according to plan. But, what happens when the solid rock you thought you were standing on suddenly feels like sinking sand? What happens when suddenly there is a shift, and one minute you are standing firm on your own two feet and the next minute you find yourself thrown to the ground by an unforeseen circumstance. Where is your praise then? I pray that even then—while it "seems" you are sinking, while it "seems" you are in the dirt—there is still praise in your heart.

> RESTRAINING YOUR PRAISE IS EVIDENCE OF DEFEAT—FIGHT THE BATTLE WITH YOUR PRAISE! PRESS ON WITH YOUR PRAISE! DECLARE VICTORY THROUGH YOUR PRAISE!

"Yeah, but you just don't know what I'm going through!" you may be saying. "I don't feel like praising God right now or anytime soon." I know, and I understand that there are some situations in life that puts us in a place where we find it difficult to muster up a word of praise. Situations such as the death of a loved one, the diagnosis of a life-threatening illness, the loss of a job, divorce, the loss of a home or assets—situations that make us angry, make us want to just curl up and disappear from the face of the earth. These are the times when the enemy wants us to shut up and curse God. These are the times when we are bombarded with thoughts like

"See, this God thing does not work" or "How can God be good if I'm going through this?" or "God is punishing me" or "Why me, Lord? I've been faithful to you. Why me?" These are the times when suddenly all the unbelievers around us "seem" to be prospering while we are barely getting by. These are the times when not even a whisper of praise is able to flow from our lips. But, these are *also* the times when we must push past our natural emotions and praise God anyhow. Restraining your praise is evidence of defeat—fight the battle with your praise! Press on with your praise! Declare victory through your praise!

Our praise is the external evidence of our faith in God and His Word—having faith that "all things work together for good to those who love God, to those who are the called according to His purpose" (Romans 8:28), believing and trusting that "His grace is sufficient for us, for His strength is made perfect in our weakness" (2 Corinthians 12:9). Through praise we speak victory into existence. Praising refreshes our souls with freshly squeezed doses of God's goodness, grace, love, and strength; renewing our spirits in times of difficulty.

There is nothing on the face of the earth that God is not able to deliver us from. "God is faithful to His Word and to His compassionate nature, and He can be trusted not to let you be tempted and tried and assayed beyond your ability and strength of resistance and power to endure, but with the temptation He will always also provide the way out; the means of escape to a landing place, that you may be capable and strong and powerful to bear up under it patiently"

(1 Corinthians 10:13 AMP). Our trials are not surprises to God. He is *not* shocked when we are facing difficult times or disastrous situations. He knew they were coming our way. But we must find comfort in knowing that in every trial we face, God has already put in place our victory. If He brought you to it, He knew you were stronger than the situation, and He is faithful, by nature, to bring you through it. And that's a reason to praise!

> IF WE JUST TAKE THE TIME TO LOOK BACK AT ALL THAT GOD HAS DONE FOR US, WE WILL FIND A REASON TO HAVE PRAISE IN OUR HEARTS AND ON OUR LIPS.

How many times have you faced a situation where you thought you would never make it through, where you thought, "There is no coming back from this"? But God. How many times have you thought, "This is it!" only to discover that it was just the start of a new beginning? Life does not guarantee us that there will be no pains, no struggles, no tragedies, no despair—let's leave that for the movies. Being a believer, saved, sanctified, and filled with the Holy Ghost, is not the golden ticket to the easy life. But, if we just take the time to look back at all that God has done for us, we will find a reason to have praise in our hearts and on our lips.

Look back at the moments when you thought you would have never made it through—but God! Look back at the days and nights spent in turmoil—but God! "Remember the days of old; meditate on all His works, muse on the work of His hands" (Psalm 134:5). Look back and see the goodness of

God. Look back and see His mercies. Look back and see all He has done. Look back and see all He has brought you through. When we simply look back, we will always have a reason to praise.

Praise God despite all that you may go through; have praise in your heart and on your lips. When we are grieving, He comforts us like no other. When we are sick, He heals us like no other. When we are financially burdened, He is faithful to deliver us like no other. And when we just don't feel like we can make it any further, He is faithful to carry us through. God is love, and His love for us shelters us, delivers us, protects us, and keeps us. His love lifts us out of the deepest valley, stretches over the widest sea, finds us in our hiding places and brings us into His glorious light. Selah. Hallelujah!

SACRIFICE OF PRAISE

"Let us continually offer the sacrifice of praise to God, that is, the fruit of our lips, giving thanks to His name" (Hebrew 13:15). Praise God in the middle of the storm, praise Him in the midst of the headache, heartache, and disappointment. In all that we go through, we must offer up a sacrifice of praise. The Psalmist says: "I will freely sacrifice to You; I will praise your name, O Lord, for it is good. For He has delivered me out of all trouble

> THERE ARE NO, ABSOLUTELY NO CIRCUMSTANCES THAT GOD IS NOT ABLE TO DELIVER US FROM.

and my eye has seen its desire upon my enemies" (Psalm 54:6-7). When we praise in the middle of what seems to be a dire situation, our praise becomes the weapon that confuses and defeats our enemies. When it seems like we are down and out for the count, our praise in faith wins us the victory. See every trial as an opportunity to offer up a sacrifice of praise to God, to execute your faith through praise.

Praise must *not* be contingent upon whether or not we are going through good times or bad times. We must "bless the Lord at all times; let His praise continually be in our mouths" (Psalm 34:1) because the "Lord is good" (Psalm 135:3), despite our circumstances. Praise God in faith, knowing that regardless of what we face in life, He is Abba Father and He is always for us. Despite what we may have done in our lives, He is never against us.

When the enemy bombards us with the thought of being "realistic," suggesting that our complete faith and trust in God is unrealistic, simply resist, renounce, rebuke, and offer up a sacrifice of praise to God. There are no, absolutely no circumstances that God is not able to deliver us from. The Lord God "has made the heavens and the earth by His great power and outstretched arm. There is nothing too hard for Him" (Jeremiah 32:17). God can do all things *but* fail. Praise God!

SEASONS OF PRAISE

"To everything there is a season, to everything there is a season, a time for every purpose under heaven. A time to be born, and a time to die; a time to plant, and a time to pluck what is planted; a time to kill, and a time to heal; a time to break down, and a time to build up; a time to weep, and a time to laugh; a time to mourn, and a time to dance; a time to cast away stones, and a time to gather stones; a time to embrace, and a time to refrain from embracing; a time to gain, and a time to lose; a time to keep, and a time to throw away; a time to tear, and a time to sew; a time to keep silence, and a time to speak; a time to love, and a time to hate; a time of war, and a time of peace" (Ecclesiastes 3:1-8). There is a reason for every season in our lives, and in this season, you may be one praise away from receiving your victory.

> IT IS IN THIS SEASON OF PAIN AND PRESSURE THAT HE IS GIVING YOU THE STRENGTH TO BUILD SPIRITUAL MUSCLES.

Oftentimes our praises are hindered because we think we have God all figured out. We think we know all His patterns and all His ways, presuming that the way He showed up last season will be the way He will show up this season. But, what we fail to realize is that our God is not a boring, monotonous God. What He did last season may not be exactly what He will do this season, and how He showed up last season may not be how He'll show up this season. "My thoughts are not your thoughts, nor are your ways my ways, says the Lord" (Isaiah 55:8).

When we think we have God all figured out, we set ourselves up for disappointment. When this season does not look like the past seasons, when things aren't going according to what we envisioned, we question, lose hope, lose faith, and lose our praise. But, praise is exactly what's needed for this season, because it is in this season that God is doing a new thing in you and through you. It is in this season—this unfamiliar season, filled with chaos—that He is taking you to a new level. It is in this season of pain and pressure that He is giving you the strength to build spiritual muscles. It is in this season of hills and valleys that He's taking you on a new journey, that He's leading you to greater heights, that He's preparing you for all He's called you to be. Your praise is the catalyst propelling you into your seasons of victories. Regardless of the season or the reason, praise God!

Praise Always

A heart of gratitude leads to a tongue of praise. "Praise the Lord, for the Lord is good; sing praises to His name, for it is pleasant" (Psalm 135:3). God dwells in the praises of His people; He finds pleasure in the praises of His children. Every morning we awake to see another day, there should be praise in our hearts and praise protruding from our lips.

If you have eyes to see, praise God! If you have ears to hear, praise God! If you have legs to walk with, praise God! If you have hands and fingers, praise God! If you have all your senses and faculties, praise God! If you have a sound mind, praise God! If you have a healthy body, praise God! Now, some of you may say, "Well, I'm not so healthy. I'm battling this disease and that disease." Regardless, praise God! With every breath that you take, praise God, as every breath is a gift from above.

Do not take anything for granted. God is good and deserving of all the praise. Just look at nature and you must find a reason to praise. The fact that you are not able to see the wind, but you are able to feel the cool breeze against your skin, is a reason to praise God.

> YOU WERE COUNTED OUT AND DISMISSED, BUT JESUS LIFTED YOU UP, DUSTED OFF THE DIRT FROM YOUR PAST, WASHED YOU IN HIS BLOOD, CLOTHED YOU IN HIS GLORY, DECLARED YOU WORTHY, AND MADE YOU SHINY AND NEW—SO PRAISE GOD!

Had it not been for the grace of God, so many of us would have perished a long time ago. The accident should have killed you, but you are still here today, so praise God! The addiction should have killed you, but you are here today, so praise God! The disease should have killed you, but you are still here today, so praise God! You should be homeless, but you have a roof over your head, so praise God! The abuse should have killed you, but you're still here, so praise God! The struggles and battles should have killed you, but you are still here, so praise God! You were counted out and dismissed, but Jesus lifted you up, dusted off the dirt from your past, washed you in His blood, clothed you in His glory, declared you worthy, and made you shiny and new—so praise God!

"Praise the lord! Praise the lord from the heavens; Praise Him in the heights!" (Psalm 148:1). "Praise Him, all His angels; Praise Him, all His hosts!" (Psalm 148:2). "Praise Him with loud cymbals; Praise Him with clashing cymbals!" (Psalm 150:5). "Praise Him for His mighty acts; Praise Him according to His excellent greatness!" (Psalm 150:2). "Praise the Lord! Praise the name of the Lord; Praise Him, O you servants of the Lord!" (Psalm 135:1). "Praise Him with the sound of the trumpet; Praise Him with the lute and harp!" (Psalm 150:3). "Praise Him with the timbrel and dance; Praise Him with stringed instruments and flutes!" (Psalm 150:4). "Praise Him, sun and moon; Praise Him, all you stars of light!" (Psalm 148:3). "Praise the Lord from the earth" (Psalm 148:7); "Let everything that has breath praise the Lord. Praise the Lord!" (Psalm 150:6).

> THERE ARE NO FORCES STRONG ENOUGH TO WITHSTAND OUR FAITH-FILLED PRAYERS, GRATITUDE, AND PRAISE.

We were created and commanded to give God praise (Psalm 148:5), to glorify His holy name, to magnify His name, to bless His name and speak of His mercies, goodness, and love all the days of our lives. Praise God with your song, praise Him with your dance—praise the Lord, all ye saints! Faith-filled praises precede victories—so praise God! Hallelujah!

ARSENAL OF VICTORIES

Pray and receive your victory. Offer thanksgiving and receive your victory. Praise and receive your victory. There are no forces strong enough to withstand our faith-filled prayers, gratitude, and praise. Faithfully combined, they are the powerful arsenal of victories—the unbeatable weapons of spiritual combat guaranteed to triumph, securing us life's victories. With prayer, gratitude, and praise, the battle has already been won. Receive your victory today in Jesus' name!

MAKE YOUR OWN NOTES

What is your prayer and worship life like?

_____
_____
_____
_____
_____
_____

> "I WILL BLESS THE LORD AT ALL TIMES; HIS PRAISE SHALL CONTINUALLY BE IN MY MOUTH."
>
> ~ PSALM 34:1

_____
_____
_____
_____
_____
_____
_____

POCKET
9

BLESSED VESSELS

One of the most fulfilling things in life is being a blessing to someone else. I live to bless—it gives me great pleasure to do something for someone, to encourage someone, to help someone in need. There is no greater feeling than the feeling that I get from helping a fellow human being.

I've always known that I wanted to do something that would bless many people. As a child, I was so inspired by Dr. Martin Luther King Jr., and oftentimes I would fantasize about fighting against injustice and helping someone else, regardless of race, culture, gender, or age. I have always had a deep, passionate desire to inspire and motivate others. But as I got older, those passions took a backseat to my desires to "make it big!" Sure, it was still on my agenda—I even practiced my inspirational speeches once or twice in the shower—but all that was to come *after* the major successes. Needless to say, "a man's heart plans his way, but the Lord directs his steps" (Proverbs 16:9).

> I'VE MADE IT MY LIFE'S PURPOSE TO BLESS, TO INSPIRE, TO ENCOURAGE, TO MOTIVATE, AND TO BE A LIGHT IN THIS DARK WORLD. AND, CHILDREN OF GOD, YOU ARE CALLED TO DO THE SAME.

After my encounter with the Light and while still hospitalized, I began to pray for a purposeful life. One evening as I sat on my hospital bed, watching one of my favorite shows, *Extreme Makeover: Home Edition,* God spoke into my spirit about a nonprofit organization. I quickly grabbed the only thing I had to write on, a napkin, and began writing down the entire concept. Now, I had never worked in the nonprofit industry and really had no knowledge of how to structure one. But, on that faithful evening, God gave me the entire concept from beginning to end.

After being discharged from the hospital, I still thought about the nonprofit, but I decided that I would create it *after* I completed the work I started before my initial hospitalization. You see, that was a "for-profit," and I knew that it was going to be big! But, again, men make plans and God laughs.

It was not until I embarked on my spiritual journey that I began to really think about the nonprofit organization. So one morning, I asked God what He wanted me to do: "Lord should I continue with this for-profit or should I work on this nonprofit?" The minute I said "nonprofit," I felt God's indescribable peace. But that still wasn't enough for me; I had to make sure. "Lord, for-profit?" I asked, and felt this uneasy feeling. "Hmm, that's strange. Never felt that way about it before," I thought. "Lord, nonprofit?" I asked, and was again immediately filled with His sweet, indescribable peace. Then God spoke into my heart and said, "Everything you've prayed to me for is in this nonprofit. You've prayed to be a blessing, you've prayed to be creative, and you've prayed to be involved in business." Overwhelmed by His love, I didn't know what to do, except to cry and thank Him.

As I lay there, still in shock, I turned to my left in a daze, and God spoke into my spirit and said, "Look at what I am showing you." As I focused my eyes, I saw in front of me an article that I had ripped out and pinned onto my vision board. The heading read, "How to Start a Nonprofit Organization." Needless to say, I was again overwhelmed.

Since then, I've made it my life's purpose to bless, to inspire, to encourage, to motivate, and to be a light in this dark world. And, children of God, you are called to do the same.

Called to Bless

You may be now seeing the victories manifested in your life, and I am excited for you! You may be experiencing supernatural breakthroughs. Your faith may be increasing daily. You pray, give thanks, praise, and speak life daily, and you're simply living victoriously. Now, what else could there possibly be? Well, it seems that the only thing left to do is to be a blessing—to bless others. Well, what did you think? Did you think that this was all about you and what you wanted? I am so sorry, but actually this was never really about you. Yes, of course God wants you to prosper and live victoriously, but not for selfish reasons. The purpose of being blessed is so that you can be a blessing. You are blessed *only* to be a blessing.

> WHEN WE CHOOSE SELFLESS LIVING — A LIFE COMMITTED TO BEING A BLESSING — WE BECOME GLORY CARRIERS, THE ESSENCE OF CHRIST'S LOVE.

Jesus was the epitome of a Servant of God. His earthly

ministry epitomized what it meant to truly serve others, and His life was the greatest example of selfless living. Christ never ceased or grew weary of "doing good" (Acts 10:38): healing the sick, feeding the hungry, mending broken hearts, delivering the oppressed from spiritual bondage, and so much more. He eventually gave of Himself in the most selfless act ever recorded in the history of humankind—He gave up His earthly life, dying for us, that through Him we may be reconciled as children of God and given the gift of eternal life.

As believers, we must fashion our lives the way Christ lived while on earth. Now, please do not misinterpret me: I am in no way suggesting that you voluntarily give up your physical life for another person, or allow someone to misuse you or abuse you for the sake of love. What I am saying is that we are called to "be imitators of God in everything we do. Walking in love, following the example of Christ, as He loved us and has given Himself for us" (Ephesians 5:1-2). Therefore, every act of giving, every kind gesture, every blessing bestowed upon another is an imitation of the love of Christ for us and in us.

We must choose to die to self; we must choose to give up selfish desires and self-serving motives for the benefit and edification of another. It is the act of doing good, sharing, and "serving one another through love" (Galatians 5:13) that pleases God (Hebrew 13:16). When we choose selfless living—a life committed to being a blessing—we become glory carriers, the essence of Christ's love.

There are so many ways we can serve God and be a

blessing to one another. Oftentimes we think that the act of blessing starts and ends with our family, but we are called to serve our extended families as well—to serve the church, to serve our communities, to serve our nation and the world. We each have a role to play. We are each commissioned to be "servants of God" (Titus 1:1) and have been given "spiritual gifts" (1 Corinthians 12:1), "equipping us for the work of ministry, for the edifying of the body of Christ" (Ephesians 4:12).

As a result, we must go forth as "members of the body of Christ" (1 Corinthians 12:27) and commit ourselves to others—blessing others with our gifts, talents, interests, and finances. When we willfully and faithfully embrace the act of giving, we will not only have spiritually, emotionally, and psychologically fulfilling lives but "our gifts will return to us in full—pressed down, shaken together to make room for more, running over, and poured into our laps" (Luke 6:38 NLT). "He who gathered much had nothing left over, and he who gathered little had no lack" (2 Corinthians 8:15). There is victory in giving, serving, and being a blessing.

> CHRIST HAS GIVEN YOU A SPIRITUAL GIFT, AND ITS PURPOSE WILL ALWAYS BE FOR THE BENEFIT OF ANOTHER AND FOR THE EDIFICATION OF THE BODY OF CHRIST.

GIVING BACK WITH OUR SPIRITUAL GIFTS

Spiritual gifts are the supernatural talents, skills, and abilities of the Holy Spirit, "distributed to each believer individually according to His will" (1 Corinthians 12:11). "There are different kinds of spiritual gifts, but the same Spirit is the source of them all. There are different kinds of service, but we serve the same Lord. God works in different ways, but it is the same God who does the work in all of us. A spiritual gift is given to each of us so we can help each other. To one person the Spirit gives the ability to give wise advice; to another the same Spirit gives a message of special knowledge. The same Spirit gives great faith to another, and to someone else the one Spirit gives the gift of healing. He gives one person the power to perform miracles, and another the ability to prophesy. He gives someone else the ability to discern whether a message is from the Spirit of God or from another spirit. Still another person is given the ability to speak in unknown languages, while another is given the ability to interpret what is being said" (1 Corinthians 12:4-10 NLT). Regardless of the gift, it is important that you are aware that Christ has given you a spiritual gift, and that its purpose will always be for the benefit of another and for the edification of the body of Christ.

As we become increasingly aware of our spiritual gifts and as we mature in these gifts, we must seek to find opportunities to serve, opportunities to utilize our gifts. Now, we know that we are not all called to be on the pulpit, but there are many ways we can serve. For instance, you may be an optimist; you've always been a positive individual. But now that you belong to Christ, your faith has grown tremendously. You walk and live by faith daily, always expecting God to do great things in your life and the life of others. To you may be given "faith by the Spirit," and with that you may seek to serve as an intercessor, faithfully interceding for others through prayers. Or, you may be called to encourage others to live faithfully. It may be that you have always been a fast learner—breaking down complex applications and information has always come easily for you. To you may be given the "gift of wisdom," and with that you may choose to serve by volunteering as a teacher. Now, you may not want to teach in a classroom setting, but you could volunteer to lead a church group or a community group. You could even volunteer to teach a life-skills class in an underserved community. Regardless of what your spiritual gifts are, they will only serve to supernaturally enhance that which God has already placed inside of you. See your gifts, acknowledge your gifts, and use your gifts to bless the lives of others.

> SEE YOUR GIFTS, ACKNOWLEDGE YOUR GIFTS, AND USE YOUR GIFTS TO BLESS THE LIVES OF OTHERS.

If you just don't think that you have any gifts, maybe you are just not able to pinpoint any particular gift, I suggest that you ask God to reveal them to you. Pray for clarity, understanding, and the development of your gift or gifts. And as you mature spiritually, choose to honor God through service—serving within your church, serving your neighbors, serving your community, and serving wherever the Spirit leads you.

GIVING BACK THROUGH TITHES AND OFFERINGS

There are so many ways that we can serve and be a blessing. One of those ways is through our financial gifts—yes, money! You may be saying, "Oh, I knew she would have to mention money!" But, before you shrug your shoulders, and put up the mental stop sign, let me say: I get it. I understand that the financial aspect of giving is not one that most of us like to talk about. We don't mind giving of ourselves through time and energy, but when it comes to the mighty dollar...well, that's another story. But, as children of God we must give of ourselves financially, and it must always start and continue with our house of worship, the church.

The concept of tithing and offerings makes many of us uncomfortable: "Why do I have to give ten percent? Pastor looks like He's doing better than I am!" For some reason, we have been deceived to believe that the sheer act of tithing and offerings is an act that serves to increase the wealth of our pastors. Instead of considering it a biblical mandate, we see it as a ploy to line the pockets of the leaders of the church. There is even a misconception that we no longer have to tithe or make offerings simply because Christ has implemented a new covenant. But, child of God, the fact is that tithing is biblical—it always has been and always will be, and Christ himself approved it.

In Luke 11:42 (NLT), Jesus said, "You *should* tithe, yes, but do not neglect justice and the love of God." Again, this is why it is so imperative that we, believers in Christ, read, meditate, and understand the Word of God for ourselves. Not knowing the Word may mean the difference between a life of lack and a life of abundance, a life that honors and pleases God and a life that dishonors and displeases Him, a life of defeats and a life of victories.

TITHING AND OFFERING

Despite the misconception, tithing is in no way giving to the church. It is the act of giving back to God a portion of the blessings He has bestowed upon us through our income. It is a biblical order implemented by God to the children of Israel: "You shall offer up a heave offering of it to the Lord, a tenth of the tithe" (Numbers 18:26); "The Levites shall bring up a tenth of the tithes to the house of our God, to the rooms of the storehouse" (Nehemiah 10:38). It was and still is the means by which we acknowledge that all that we have belongs to God. It is "He who gives us power to get wealth" (Deuteronomy 8:18), and so we offer up a tenth of our income as a thanksgiving offering to God for all He has done for us.

> IT IS THROUGH OUR TITHES AND OFFERINGS THAT THE CHURCH IS ABLE TO FUNCTION EFFECTIVELY WHILE MEETING THE SPIRITUAL, PHYSICAL, AND EMOTIONAL NEEDS OF ITS MEMBERS AND THE COMMUNITY AT LARGE.

God is so good to us. He is full of grace, love, and mercy. Out tithing is an outward expression of our appreciation for God's goodness and our desire to honor Him. It should *not* be considered a burden or a scam by the leaders of the church. Instead, it should be a "freewill offering" (Deuteronomy 12:7), rooted in our desires to give back to a God who has given us so much.

An offering is anything given *above* the ten percent required for tithing. It may be anything from a dime to a million dollars, and it too is a freewill offering, honored in the sight of God. Malachi 3:10 tells us, "Bring all the tithes into the storehouse, that there may be food in My house." The House of God is the sanctuary—the church—and what better way is there to please and honor God than to build up His sanctuary through our faithful giving?

The House of God is where we come together and collectively feed off the presence of God. It is one of the ways by which we receive our daily bread—the Word of God. It is where we find fellowship, "forsaking not the assembling of ourselves together" (Hebrews 10:25). The House of God is our home away from home. Through the power of the Holy Spirit, it gives comfort, it delivers, it heals, it sets free, and so much more. It is through our tithes and offerings that the church is able to function effectively while meeting the spiritual, physical, and emotional needs of its members and the community at large.

"Will a man rob God? Yet you have robbed Me! But you say, in what way have we robbed You? In tithes and offerings" (Malachi 3:8). Feeding from the House of God while neglecting to give tithes and offerings is considered robbery in the eyes of God. Now this may sound harsh, but think about it: If we truly believe that all that we have belongs to God;

that it is through His grace that we have what we have, yet still, we withhold from Him the tenth of which He requires from us, then obviously we are guilty of robbery! We should all be so happy that God is not like man; otherwise most of us would be locked away in misery and poverty with no hope of release.

God is not man. He is good and merciful, and it all belongs to Him. Be thankful that He does not require fifty percent, thirty percent, or even twenty percent of our income. He simply desires for us to honor Him and to build and maintain His sanctuary with our offerings and ten percent of what He has blessed us with. "But I don't have anything to give," you may be saying. You may not have income to tithe, but if you have a dime, give it as an offering. When you give from your heart, God is faithful to honor it.

> WHEN WE OFFER UP TO GOD OUR TITHES AND OFFERINGS, WE ARE ESSENTIALLY SOWING SEEDS INTO THE KINGDOM OF GOD, SOWING IN "FERTILE SOIL."

God will not twist your arm to receive what already belongs to Him; the choice is yours to give. But know that "he who sows sparingly will also reap sparingly, and he who sows bountifully will also reap bountifully. So let each one give as he purposes in his heart, not grudgingly or of necessity, for God loves a cheerful giver" (2 Corinthians 9:6-7).

REAP THROUGH GIVING

In the Kingdom of God there are sow, time, and harvest

seasons. When we offer up to God our tithes and offerings, we are essentially sowing seeds into the Kingdom of God, sowing in "fertile soil" (Matthew 13:8). Now, the natural evolution of anything sown is the physical manifestation of the seed. Our tithes and offerings are seeds. The goal of the enemy is to place fear, distrust, and unbelief in our hearts in order to prevent us from giving to God that which is rightfully His. "If I give this, I won't have anything left," we might say, or "I don't believe I need to do this. This is just for the pastor's pocket" or "When I give this, I'm the one that's left without." Children of God, resist, renounce, rebuke, renew, and have faith!

When we choose to walk by faith and not by sight, when we choose to walk in obedience, when we choose to bring our tithes and offerings to the House of God, He promises to "open the windows of heaven and pour out a blessing so great that we won't have enough room to take it in" (Malachi 3:10 NLT). When we are faithful to give of ourselves financially, with tithes and offerings, "God will generously provide all our needs and we will always have everything we need and plenty left over to share with others" (2 Corinthians 9:8 NLT). When we bless the House of God, He promises that "all nations will call us blessed" (Malachi 3:10-12). These are but a few of His promises to us, and they are true and proven.

Have faith in God, serve Him, and honor Him with your tithe and offerings. For every seed sown in the House of God will not fail to bring forth "a harvest of thirty, some sixty, and some a hundred" (Mark 4:20) folds. Have faith. Sow your tithes and offerings, and in time you will reap an abundant harvest of victories!

Always a Blessing

As we continue to grow and spiritually mature in Christ, we must also continue serving and striving always to be a blessing to others. This may at times be difficult, because unfortunately we live in a self-serving world, a world that says, "Hold on to all you have," "Save, save, save, and give nothing away," "Nothing in life is free," "You don't pay me, then I can't do anything for you" and so on. We live in a dog-eat-dog world, but let me remind you, children of God, that "our citizenship is in heaven" (Philippians 3:20). And as such, we are strangers in a foreign land who live, move, and have our beings in Christ. We do not live by the world's system; we live by the Word of God. The same Word that tells us to "be rich in good works, ready to give and willing to share" (1 Timothy 6:18). The same Word that promises us that when we give, "we will receive" (Luke 6:38 NLT). We trust in the Word of God, which promises us that "he who gives to the poor will not lack" (Proverbs 28:27). We believe the Word, which tells us that "he who has a generous eye will be blessed, for he gives of his bread to the poor" (Proverbs 22:9).

> WE WERE NOT PLACED ON THE EARTH TO BE SELFISH HOARDERS OF EARTHLY GOODS, BUT WE ARE CALLED TO BE A BLESSING, TO GIVE BACK AND BLESS THE LIFE OF ANOTHER IN WHATEVER WAY WE CAN.

We must keep in mind that "we are His workmanship, created in Christ Jesus for good works" (Ephesians 2:10), called and commissioned to "not grow weary in doing good" (2 Thessalonians 3:13). We can be confident that when we "do good and share with those in need, these are the sacrifices that pleases God" (Hebrew 13:16 NLT).

Remember: Our blessings are not only for our benefit or exclusively for our family's benefit; they are also for our extended family—people we may cross paths with on a daily basis or neighbors in need. As children of God, we are called to be a blessing to our families, churches, neighbors, communities, and nation.

RICH FOOL

The parable of the Rich Fool in Luke 12:13-21 is a great lesson about what happens when we focus on ourselves and feed our own selfish desires. The parable begins with a rich man who has so much wealth that he does not have enough room to store his overflow. If he were alive today, he would probably be on *Forbes*'s "World's Richest People" list—yes, that kind of rich! But what makes this man a "fool" is the fact that he does not recognize that all he has is the result of God's blessing, and that he was given the overflow so that he could be a blessing to someone else. He is so selfish that he decides to tear down his barns and build bigger barns to store all of his goods—it is obviously all about him! He does not stop to consider maybe the poor farmer down the road who is struggling to provide for his family, or the beggar who sits at his gate hoping for a little alms to make it through the day. No, he considers no one but himself. This "rich fool" fails to walk in God's core principle of love—"love your neighbor as yourself" (Matthew 19:19). He chooses to "store up treasures here on earth, where moths eat them and rust destroys them, and where thieves break in and steal" (Matthew 6:19 NLT), as opposed to giving to the needy, sharing with others, and being a blessing to someone else. He is self-centered and self-serving, and at the end, he dies that very night with no one to leave his worldly goods to.

Do you know anyone like that? This man reminds me of the stories we hear from time to time, stories about these "well-to-do" folks who live in seclusion, the ones who "generously" give a fifty-cent tip to everyone who serves them and a dollar during the holiday season: "Here's a little something for you and your family," they say. They are the ones who hide millions of dollars under their beds or in some secret place in their homes, the ones who leave millions of dollars to their cats and not a penny to a person in need. But in Luke 12:15; 21 Jesus warns us to "take heed and beware of covetousness (greed), for one's life does not consist in the abundance of the things he possesses. He who lays up treasure for himself, and is not rich toward God."

> CHRIST IS THE BEST, MOST PRECIOUS, "INDESCRIBABLE GIFT" YOU WILL EVER HAVE THE PLEASURE OF GIVING TO YOUR FELLOW HUMAN BEING.

Now, let me clarify: I am in no way advocating for you to

go out and give everything away or sell all your possessions. We are also required to be faithful stewards over the blessings. But, we are commissioned to give of ourselves, one to another, with the full understanding that "it is more blessed to give than to receive" (Acts 20:35). We were not placed on the earth to be selfish hoarders of earthly goods, but we are called to be a blessing, to give back and bless the life of another in whatever way we can.

KEEP IT GOING

So, whom have you blessed today, apart from your immediate family members? Each day we should seek to be a blessing to someone in one way or another.

You do not have to be financially wealthy to be a blessing. Give a word of encouragement to someone today; speak life into someone else's situation today; volunteer to teach a class in your community today; inspire someone through your talents today; give a donation to a cause that's near and dear to your heart today; visit someone in the hospital today; lift someone up in prayer today; hug someone today; start a scholarship fund today; volunteer with an organization today; listen attentively to someone today; put a smile on someone's face today; be selfless today. But most importantly, introduce someone to Jesus Christ today.

Christ is the best, most precious, "indescribable gift" you will ever have the pleasure of giving to your fellow human being. Jesus is the gift that keeps on giving and giving and giving.

Remember, you are blessed only to be a blessing! Choose to be a blessing today, and know that the victory is all yours in Jesus's name!

MAKE YOUR OWN NOTES

Are you focused on serving or are you more concerned with being served?

> "GIVE AND IT WILL BE GIVEN TO YOU: GOOD MEASURE, PRESSED DOWN, SHAKEN TOGETHER, AND RUNNING OVER WILL BE PUT IN YOUR BOSOM."
>
> ~ LUKE 6:38

POCKET 10

CLOSING REMARKS

So I've finally figured out my place and my space in God's plan. It took me a while. I had to go through some valleys and some rocky terrains, but if given the opportunity, I would not change what happened for anything. Why? Because through it all I found freedom, through it all I found purpose, through it all I found peace, through it all I found joy, through it all I found love, and through it all I found Jesus. Now, I can't say that I've figured it all out—definitely not! Every day is an opportunity to learn, grow, develop, and mature in Christ.

> I PRAY THAT YOU REALIZE THAT THIS IS NOT ABOUT RELIGION—IT IS ABOUT DEVELOPING AN INTIMATE RELATIONSHIP WITH GOD.

I pray, child of God, that as you continue on this wonderful journey with Christ, you will stand up tall and be bold in your knowledge that you have been born-again into the royal family of Jesus Christ. I pray that you realize that this is not about religion—it is about developing an intimate relationship with God. I pray that you will go forth and live victoriously in Christ with the full understanding that everything God promises in His Word is for you to have.

I pray that you have chosen to release yourself from the shackles of your past through forgiveness. I encourage you to renew your mind, speak life, walk in the Spirit, and have faith and trust in God, regardless of anything you may go through. Believe, child of God, that God has anointed you for great works. Pray, be thankful, and praise Him at all times.

Know that you are blessed and choose to be a blessing.

In closing, I pray child of God, that you will experience supernatural victories in every area of your life. That the love of Jesus Christ fills your heart, overtakes your life and blesses you beyond measure. You are one of His marvelous masterpieces, finely crafted and uniquely built. Go forth fully assured that God loves you unconditionally and will continue to love you. Your life is in His hands, trust Him, believe Him and live victoriously through Him. God bless you!

www.ingramcontent.com/pod-product-compliance
Lightning Source LLC
LaVergne TN
LVHW041611070426
835507LV00008B/194